Off by Heart

Performing and presenting poetry
in the primary school

Linda Pagett and John Somers

Acknowledgements

We would like to thank the many people who helped make this book. Their patience, energy, generosity and creativity are a tribute to the work undertaken in our schools:

The staff and pupils at Drake's Primary School, East Budleigh, especially Headteacher Jane Griffiths and teachers Fiona Ludlow, Debra Eveleigh, Sarah Hopkins and Eileen Pye.

Rob Bennett, Paul Moger-Taylor and Tony Ovens from the Faculty of Education (Rolle), University of Plymouth. Jon Primrose from the School of Performance Arts, University of Exeter.

Tony Ovens took the photographs.

We are grateful to the following who have kindly granted permission for the use of copyright material:

Bully Night' and 'Cousin Nell' by Roger McGough, from *You Tell Me*, Puffin, 1981. Copyright © Roger McGough. Reprinted with permission of Peters Fraser & Dunlop on behalf of Roger McGough; 'My Sister Laura' and 'Granny' by Spike Milligan, from *Funny folk and other poems about people*, Faber and Faber, 1986. Reprinted by permission of Spike Milligan Productions Limited; 'My Dad, Your Dad' by Kit Wright. Reprinted by permission of the Authors Licensing & Collecting Society Ltd on behalf of Kit Wright; 'The Tickle Rhyme' by Ian Serraillier © Anne Serraillier. Reprinted with kind permission of Anne Serraillier; 'My Sister Jane' by Ted Hughes, from *Meet my Folks* by Ted Hughes, published by Faber and Faber Limited. Reprinted with permission of Faber and Faber Limited; 'Please Mrs Butler' from *Please Mrs Butler* by Allan Ahlbert, Kestrel 1983, copyright © Allan Ahlberg, 1983. Reprinted by permission of Penguin Books Ltd; 'Alone in the Grange' by Gregory Harrison. Copyright © Gregory Harrison, first published in 1971 by Oxford University Press in *The Night of the Wild Horses*. Reprinted with kind permission of the author; 'Green Man, Blue Man' by Charles Causley, from *Collected poems for children* by Charles Causley, Macmillan. Reprinted with permission of David Higham Associates; 'Mouth Open Story Jump Out' by John Agard, from *Say It Again Granny!*, published by Bodley Head, 1987. Reprinted by kind permission of John Agard c/o Caroline Sheldon Literary Agency; 'When Anancy Say' by John Agard, from *Laughter is an Egg* published by Viking, 1990. Reprinted by kind permission of John Agard c/o Caroline Sheldon Literary Agency; 'The Secret ' by Gareth Owen, © Gareth Owen 2000, c/o Rogers, Coleridge & White Ltd., 20 Powis Mews, London W11 1JN. Reprinted by kind permission of the author and Rogers, Coleridge & White Limited.

Off by Heart is published by the National Association for the Teaching of English (NATE), the UK subject teacher association for all aspects of the teaching of English from pre-school to university.

NATE, 50 Broadfield Road, Sheffield S8 OXJ

Telephone: 0114 255 5419   Fax: 0114 255 5296
email: natehq@btconnect.com
website: www.nate.org.uk

© Linda Pagett and John Somers (2004)
ISBN 1 904709 07 9

Design by DCG DESIGN; Printed by Q3 Digital / Litho

Contents

INTRODUCTION

Why bother? (Ten good reasons)

'The key to proper sharing of poems is performance'
Benton and Fox (1985)

Tom is four. He has found school a bit of a struggle. He doesn't read or write yet and follows the teacher around the class saying 'What do now?' His speech is immature. He is just about to adjust the zip on his trousers and wriggle his waistband in preparation for a poetry show. In clear tones he announces . . . 'Welcome ladies and gentlemen to the Infants' Poetry Show.' In twenty minutes he will thank all the parents for coming but before that he has work to do; listening for the cues that mean he is performing lines of poetry centre stage, joining in choruses and taking part in a tableau. He does all this with the utmost confidence. He has practised in a community of performers, a society he values and wants to be a part of.

A village hall at lunchtime: a wet walk from the school; wooden floors; trestle tables neatly stacked under the stage. Six key stage two children are working in the middle of the large space. One of them wears a beautiful flowered headdress, a memento of her role as a bridesmaid, and some old net curtains cunningly folded into the robes of *The Lady of Shalott*. She is lying dead on the floor, which is proxy for a barge. Lancelot bursts dramatically into the space

'Who is this and what is here...'

(The Lady of Shalott by Alfred Lord Tennyson)

The royal sound of cheer ceases from some year sixes in the corner. The camera rolls as a pupil videos the rehearsal, which the performers will later watch to decide what is good about their work. The teacher plays an important but understated role. The pupils are in control, with a confidence born of many poetry shows and performances. The teacher is moved by the children's innocence and commitment. As they recite the poem she can hear her mother's voice reading it to her many years before. She wonders if her mother would have heard her father's voice in it. He used to perform poems in the 1930s in a village hall rather like this one.

What is going on in these two scenarios? Teachers and children are putting a lot of energy into something they consider important. Why bother? This book attempts to answer the question with compelling evidence that performing poetry can underpin language and literacy development for all pupils, as an important part of a primary school curriculum.

Poetry is written to be spoken aloud

It is a patterning of sounds and we cannot guarantee that children hear with an 'inner ear'. Pupils need to hear poems read aloud in order to develop this; then they can inject the rhythm and cadence the poet intended. Some poems simply don't make sense if they are not read aloud. I think of Roger McGough's poem, *Potato Clock* (from 'Pie in the Sky', Penguin 1990). It is only when the pun on 'up at eight o'clock', is heard that the reader 'gets it'. Without recitation how could Auden's poem *Night Mail* possibly remind the reader of a majestic rattling locomotive or how could the young reader understand the fun of:

> *She sells seashells on the seashore*
> *The shells she sells are seashells I'm sure.*
>
> ANON

unless they stutter their way through its clever juxtaposition of sounds? Poems on the page are passive. There is no rhythm, no metre, no alliteration, for all these come from the human voice.

An important part of our literary heritage

The teacher in the village hall hears her mother's voice in *The Lady of Shalott*. How long is the chain back through her family of children learning from their parents and grandparents? It would almost certainly reach back into a time when parents couldn't read or write but carried language in their head in a way we have forgotten.

The magic web of literary heritage is spun every time teachers read poems to children, every time they chant and invent playground rhymes, every time their parents, grandparents or carers pass on poems from other times and other cultures.

Poetry invites response

Benton and Fox[1] make the point that, 'Meaning is a compound of what the poem offers and what the reader brings.' We cannot respond without imagination and imagination and empathy play an important part in learning[2]. There are concerns that 'developing the imagination is no longer seen as a central pedagogic concern. Developing the imagination has been sidelined'.[3]

---

1 *Teaching Literature 9–14* by M.Benton and G.Fox, OUP 1985

2 F.Brill in *Thinking outside the box: imagination and empathy in children's non-narrative writing*, K.Kimberley, M.Meek and J.Miller (Eds), A&C Black, 2002

3 *Literacy and the lost world of imagination* by L.Dart in *Educational Research*, 43(1) pp63–77, 2001

It is important that pupils are given opportunities to live in their imagination, to respond as critical readers if we are to avoid what Ted Hughes refers to as 'mental paralysis' engendered by a scientific style of mind taught in school as an ideal. In *The Lady of Shalott*, Anne, aged 8, adapts a dream-like presence; she flips the ends of a little peasant shawl she wears as she looks into a middle distance, walks through an imaginary cornfield and recites,

> *In the stormy east wind straining*
> *The pale yellow woods were waning*
> *The broad stream in his banks complaining*
> *Heavily the low sky raining*
>
> (See performance plan for The Lady of Shalott
> BY ALFRED LORD TENNYSON, *page 46*)

The teacher is transfixed by Anne's involvement. Although Anne's literacy skills are not exceptional, she is able to capture quite profound meanings in this enactment which she would not necessarily be able to demonstrate in 'read it/write about it' or even in 'read it/talk about it' exercises. The enactment is giving her new dimensions of expression and interpretation.

Although poetry is embedded in the National Curriculum and National Literacy Strategy there have been concerns that teachers could feel constricted by a framework which, although it purports to be interactive, is in fact dominated by literacy - pupils reading and writing without due emphasis on the interactive oral work which should underpin this. One teacher, taking part in a small-scale study into teachers' understanding of how they think literacy is developed in the classroom, said:

> *When I stopped treating the poem as a kind of exercise and started conveying my own response to it, they started to do the same thing. I wouldn't do that now ... say this is very good because she has put herself into it ... because this is not what I'm being paid to do. I'm being paid to equip these children with literacy skills.*[4]

Poetry performance is an ideal context for teachers to model response, demonstrating how poems can be read in various ways and with varied forms of presentation, which allow the reader to respond individually and imaginatively.

Listening and sequencing skills are developed by activities such as:

- joining in choruses: *their heads are green and their hands are blue*
- having characters in role for direct speech: *You're tickling my back* said the caterpillar
- adding sound effects: *The fish gave a terrible scream, AHHHHHHHHHHHH*
- using musical instruments: *the mouse ran up the clock* accompanied by steps on the xylophone keys

4 *Literacy and the lost world of imagination* by L. Dart, in *Educational Research*, 43 (1) 2001

Phonological awareness is supported

This, it is widely agreed, pupils need to develop in order to read effectively (*Phonological skills and learning to read,* by Goswami and Bryant, 1990). Phonological awareness has three developmental stages: discriminating syllables; onset and rime; and phonemes – sounds within words. Poetry provides ideal texts in which to do this. Clapping the syllables of the skipping chant *Salt mustard vinegar pepper* for example helps pupils discriminate syllables. Alliterative phrases such as

> *The burglars and the bogeymen*
> *who slink*
> *while others sleep*

or clever use of rhyme

> *the creaking and the shrieking*
> *that keep me fast awake*

both from McGough's poem *Bully Night* (see below), help children to distinguish onset and rime. Assonance, as for example in the line *Bully Night I do not like...,* supports discrimination of phonemes.

Bully Night

> *Bully night*
> *I do not like*
> *the company you keep*
> *The burglars and the bogeymen*
> *who slink*
> *while others sleep*
>
> *Bully night*
> *I do not like*
> *The noises that you make*
> *The creaking and the shrieking*
> *that keep me*
> *fast awake.*
>
> *Bully night*
> *I do not like*
> *the loneliness you bring*
> *The loneliness you bring*
> *The loneliness, the loneliness*
> *the loneliness you bring,*
> *the loneliness you bring*
> *the loneliness, the*

ROGER McGOUGH

Performance can support comprehension

Basil, a Year 6 pupil, admitted: 'I only knew that there was a boat in *The Lady of Shalott* when we did (performed) it.' Leonie had no idea what a gander was until she was called upon to wear a beak and bonnet for her part in *Goosey Goosey* even though it was a nursery rhyme she had been able to recite for many years. Poetry *per se* can say nothing. Perhaps it is only when imagination and poetry come together that anything is said or heard. Children make meaning as they devise and practise their performances: teapots short and stout, using their arms to pour out, Sir Lancelot bursting on the scene knowing how a noble knight would feel on such a night, so heavy with witch craft that the other knights cross themselves for fear.

Critical faculties are developed

If pupils appraise their own and others' interpretations, they get nearer to the many shades of meaning in a poem. This kind of reflection is essential to comprehension and is recognised in the Primary National Strategy, eg. pupils should *comment constructively on plays and performances, discussing effects and how they are achieved* (objective no.40) and in many of the objectives in the NLS framework, for example:

> **Yr 1 Term 2 T11** *to learn and recite stories and rhymes with predictable and repeated patterns*

Some objectives are often interpreted as 'read about it/write about it' activities or, at best, themes for discussion, but objectives such as:

> **Yr 6 Term 3 T4** *to comment critically on the overall impact of a poem showing how language use and themes have been developed*

could be primarily addressed through performing poems, experiencing the language use first hand and experimenting with it to try and get near to what the poet intended. The invented world between poet and reader is built upon a shared understanding. If the audience/reader/listener interacts with the poem in a way that provides insight into what the poet has 'planted' in the words, the poem expands in the way an inflatable dinghy opens up to be many times its original size. This depends on a kind of intertextuality – the meaning of the poem connects with the concerns of the listener/reader. That's why the choice of poems is so crucial, for if there is no connection, there is no meaning making.

Themes in poems, such as the witchcraft in *The Lady of Shalott*, need to be explored and illustrated to support all pupils' understanding – not just those who understand at a symbolic level. Similarly it would be difficult to understand how the objective

> **Year 6 Term 2 T5** *to analyse how messages moods feelings and attitudes are conveyed in poetry*

could be attempted without some form of performance.

Performance can support the kinæsthetic learner

Learning styles vary and many pupils learn more effectively by doing. Although poems need to be heard and teachers play an important part in reading them to pupils there is no guarantee that anyone other than the good auditory learner is learning anything, or even listening. Drama techniques such as mime, tableau, and freeze-frames can be introduced to support meaning making visually and kinæsthetically. In a freeze-frame from the poem *Please Mrs Butler* (see below) at the end of the last stanza

> *Lock yourself in a cupboard, dear.*
> *Run away to sea.*
> *Do whatever you can, my flower but don't ask me!*

the children have to consider 'How is Mrs Butler going to freeze?'
- Jane decides she will have her eyes closed because she wants to block out the children; 'It's her way of saying "Enough!"'
- Judy decides she'll be holding her hand outstretched palm first 'because that's what Miss does when she means business.'

Please Mrs Butler

Please Mrs Butler
This boy Derek Drew
Keeps copying my work, Miss.
What shall I do?

Go and sit in the hall, dear.
Go and sit in the sink.
Take your books on the roof, my lamb.
Do whatever you think.

Please Mrs Butler
This boy Derek Drew
Keeps taking my rubber, Miss.
What shall I do?

Keep it in your hand, dear.
Hide it up your vest.
Swallow it if you like, my love.
Do what you think best.

Please Mrs Butler
This boy Derek Drew
Keeps calling me rude names, Miss.
What shall I do?

Lock yourself in the cupboard, dear.
Run away to sea.
Do whatever you can, my flower.
***But* don't ask me!**

ALLAN AHLBERG

The children are using their experience of classroom life in order to make sense of the words on the page. They are using literacy skills to infer and deduce how this scene would look and sound. They are also using a high order of the fundamental purposes of language – to stand for actual experience. In order to make meaning the reader has to experience vicariously, decentre and abstract. Research into effective teachers of literacy indicates that they prioritised the creation of meaning[5].

Children with EAL can benefit

Learning substantial chunks of the language can support prediction. Mohammed quickly learnt all the verses of *Who killed Cock Robin* and then went on to teach the class some Somali rhymes. Sharing poems from different cultures can support learning about language. LeRoy gave his class confidence. Having been born in London like them, he was unable to perform John Agard poems with a Jamaican patois, but his mother was happy to come to school and demonstrate the rolling sing-song rhythm of *Mouth Open Story Jump Out* (see pages 17 and 24). The whole class chanted and practised the pronunciation and she was able to translate the saying which means (roughly) 'don't tell secrets.' Poets like Agard push the reader into patois – prompting questions of how poems should be recited and what they mean. Take the wonderful poem *When Anancy Say* (below). In order to perform this poem pupils need to know something of Anancy and the fear he engenders – they learn something of the Caribbean culture and, at an implicit level, recognise that this is another form of English where verbs behave differently.

When Anancy Say

When Anancy say walk
Yuh better run

When Anancy say talk
Yuh better dumb

When Anancy say quick
Yuh better slow

When Anancy say wet
Yuh better dry

When Anancy say true
Yuh better lie

JOHN AGARD

5 *Effective Teachers of Literacy* by Medwell J, Wray D, Poulson L, Fox R, University of Exeter, 1998

Children who need extra support with literacy have a chance to perform

They may need more time than others but can be supported into solo work by:

- whole class work – chants, recitations, joining in choruses;
- group work – being one of multiple voices, providing actions while others recite;
- paired work – reciting with a more confident pupil saying small parts of the poem e.g. direct speech;
- individual work – having more time to practise, use of a tape recorder, shorter poems.

The reluctant reader or writer is not apparent in a poetry show. The best performers are not necessarily the most literate. There are some learners who understand things better by moving with the meaning, which is why drama can be so effective. In *Frames of mind*[6], Gardner suggests that inter-personal, spatial, kinæsthetic and musical intelligences exist which could well support the performer of poems even if his linguistic intelligence was not well developed. The able language user is challenged. She may well not be the best performer.

Reading and writing are supported

Practising and performing poems can lead to effective reading and writing. Children who know poems by heart have an obvious advantage when trying to read them. There are no difficult words. The young reader can cut up poems he knows and try to reassemble them in order to develop word correspondence and an understanding of syntax and poetic form. (The link between oral literacy and school literacy is described by Barrs in 'The Tune on the page', *New Readings, Contributions to an understanding of literacy*, NFER paper).

'Reading aloud becomes a bridge between orality and literacy'

Reciting chain poems is a context for borrowing a language pattern to support composition. Children recite and rehearse so that they internalise the sound qualities and then add more lines. These can then be published – the writing supports revision and recording.

A Year two class which was experimenting with writing in this kind of way practised:

"Fire, Fire!" said Mrs Dyer
"Where, Where?" said Mrs Dare
"Up the town" said Mrs Down
"Any Damage?" said Mrs Gammage
"None at all!" said Mrs Hall.

ANON

Sitting in a circle, each child added a line to the poem:

"Where's the phone?" said Mrs Bone
"I don't know!" said Mrs Slow
"The lines are down!" said Mrs Chown

This is an explicit example but there are more subtle forces at work when we recite and internalise poetry. Poems are written to be remembered. When they are learnt by heart the child carries a rich repertoire of expressive language in its head, where language is finely wrought, does clever things and can be great fun. Moon[7] describes every poetry-loving adult he knows as having 'many islands of poetry in his or her imagination and will at times eagerly speak them aloud often with a passion informed by nostalgia,'

Poetry performance is an ideal way to involve parents

Schools are social institutions. Parents are no longer requested to stay beyond a painted line in the playground but expect to join the school community and have access to their children's work. Poetry performance shows children as joyous language users, providing feedback which can surpass the ubiquitous parents' evening with its rifling through written work and concentration on reading scores. Concern with progress in speaking and listening is often marginalised, despite the accepted premise that spoken language underpins all learning.

Fun

Poetry performance is social, it is collaborative and it is inclusive. Julie's mother told her teacher that Julie, aged 7, knew not only all her own poems but the whole of the forthcoming poetry show and performed it regularly for hapless visitors. This was despite the fact that she was rather a shy child who found relationships with others difficult. She had found a community to which she not only wanted to belong but in which she featured strongly. The nurturing of pupils' self esteem is seen as one of the primary functions of any system of education.

6   *Frames of Mind, the theory of multiple intelligences* by Gardner, Fontana Press, 1983
7   *Performing poetry* by B.Moon, English and Media Centre, 1998

CHAPTER 1

Where to begin: performing poems in the Foundation stage and Key stage one

'If you want poetry to be part of children's lives you need to start with a young baby juggling on your knee so that it becomes sensory as well as aural'
Jane, Headteacher (2003)

The child

Babies lie in cots and cradles and listen to the world. They hear sounds all around them. One sound has a special significance. It is the human voice. Individual words hardly exist in speech – instead there is a stream of sound in which the pauses are more likely to indicate hesitations for thinking time than word boundaries. The first units of sound that babies are aware of are syllables which they often repeat 'da, da, da.' As developing language users they become aware of rhyme long before they come to school. Two-year-old Sophie chants *Liz the Fiz*, a rhyme she has made herself about her sister Elizabeth.

She is lucky. By the time she gets to school she will have a rich repertoire of nursery rhymes and songs. She will have heard poetry read aloud. She will have been sung to, rocked and danced with. Adults will have encouraged her to listen and respond to nursery rhymes, mime the actions of *Incy Wincy Spider*, sing and sit down suddenly in a game of *Ring a Ring a Roses*. She will be well on her way to performing poems, but for some children the first time they do this will be at school.

The teacher

It is essential that the teacher is enthusiastic about poetry and provides an environment where poems can be seen and heard. The teacher needs to model response including an understanding of how the poem can be read effectively.

It is possible to read poems in different ways with different interpretations and children need to be aware of this if they are to respond imaginatively rather than just copy the teacher.

Engagement in performance is linked to the ownership of the poem:

there is no one way to read it. Traditionally, the teacher has been the conduit through which knowledge passes to the student. This implies a state of teacher wisdom and student ignorance. Performing poetry requires a more democratic relationship between the pupil, knowledge and the teacher so that pupils' ideas are valued and acted upon. They can then see many of their creative responses embodied in the final presentation. This has implications for time, space and a need for supportive friends so that pupils can collaborate.

The teacher director

When working with reception and year one children it may be better to start with short poems, which the teacher reads and then hands over a line at a time. Children can be supported in their listening skills by standing in line as they recite; the teacher having modelled a poem can ask for volunteers for the first line, second etc. Each time someone joins the line the poem is practised from the beginning. This slowly builds up the poem and gives the teacher the chance to audition for each line analysing important features of pupil responses:

Darren speaks very clearly;
Amelia says this part in just the way an old man might speak;
Judith puts real expression in here;
Anne really looks frightened when she says this.

As pupils develop as performers they are able to work with longer poems. Narrative poems can be an appropriate choice as, initially, the teacher can act as narrator, gradually handing over parts to pupils.

For example, David, a Year 2 teacher, decided to teach Edward Lear's poem *The Jumblies* (see page 25) in which there are many examples of direct speech, including several instances where the Jumblies cry out in chorus. An initial reading by David was followed by discussion. Unfamiliar words such as 'sieve' were explored and David encouraged the children to tell the story in groups in their own words using multiple copies of the text. In a re-reading, the children chanted the chorus:

Far and few, far and few,
Are the lands where the Jumblies live;
Their heads are green and their hands are blue

one confident performer added as a solo voice

And they went to sea in a sieve.

At a further rereading, parts of direct speech were allotted to solo performers and groups and eventually David handed over the narration to a pupil so that he became teacher-director.

The group

Any cooperation and public sharing requires an atmosphere of trust in the group.

Children will be less willing to volunteer thoughts and feelings about a poem if they are unsure of the reception they will receive, or worse, expect that their contemporaries will scorn their contributions. One of the teacher's main tasks is to engender an atmosphere that allows children to feel safe enough to give freely to the development of creative work. This involves making explicit expectations about treating others and their ideas with respect and producing a positive social climate in which all can thrive.

Approaches to performance

Young children do not have the sophisticated skills to perform poetry as they read it. The skimming and scanning involved are too difficult and can inhibit any dramatic presentation or movement. As pupils begin to learn poems off by heart there are various approaches to performance. The following examples are suggestions which all relate to the National Literacy Strategy objectives.

Chanting and clapping

Humans seem to need to chant and clap. These actions are deeply embedded in many cultures particularly at times of celebration or to express emotion as a group. Think of the frenzied football crowd, willing their team to victory or Hare Krishna adherents joyfully dancing down

NLS:

Reception T10 re-read and recite stories and rhymes with predictable and repeated patterns

Year 1 Term 2 T11 to learn and recite simple poems and rhymes with actions

Year 2 Term 1 T7 to learn, re-read and recite favourite poems

PNS:

Speaking, Listening, Learning Nos. 2, 9, 13, 20

Oxford Street. Children naturally enjoy chanting and clapping in the playground as part of play:

> *One potato*
>
> *Two potatoes*
>
> *Three potatoes*
>
> *Four*
>
> *Five potatoes*
>
> *Six potatoes*
>
> *Seven potatoes*
>
> *More*

ANON

This traditional poem can be chanted in many ways:

- read the poem with a solo performer for the first word of every line and the class chanting *potatoes*;
- add an unpitched instrument to emphasise the first word of each line; class chant and clap the syllables of *pot-a-toes*;
- invite eight children to stand in line and recite a line each; extend to multiple voices so that the poem builds from a solo performer of line one, two performers of line two. . . to eight performers of line 8;
- omit words so that the performance is a mixture of instruments and clapping.

Sometimes it is more effective to chant just part of the poem, for example this lovely chorus:

> *Mouth open*
>
> *Story jump out*
>
> *Mouth open*
>
> *Story jump out*

(See page 24 for complete text of poem. See also ref. on page 11.)

- divide the class in two so that half chant *mouth open* with mouths wide open and the others echo *story jump out* as they jump up from a sitting position. This has a rolling rhythm with real opportunity to inject a patois pronunciation – Afro Caribbean pupils, parents or teachers could demonstrate how this should sound, were John Agard to read it;
- model how to read verses with wheedling, offended and peeved intonation, and then pass to a volunteer;
- chant chorus with the whole class.

Borrowing sayings or proverbs to chant to introduce and end a poem can be effective. An example is 'Bambalitty Bam Bam', a West Indian saying which roughly translated means 'I'm going to tell on you.' This could introduce the previous poem. In this arrangement the rhythm is clapped before the words are added dramatically in the last line:

> *Bam Ba Litty Bam Bam*   *(one pupil claps)*
> *Bam Ba Litty Bam Bam*   *(two pupils clap)*
> *Bam Ba Litty Bam Bam*   *(three pupils clap)*
> *Bam Ba Litty Bam Bam*   *(four pupils clap)*
> *Bam Ba Litty Bam Bam*   *(class claps)*
> *Bam Ba Litty Bam Bam*   *(class chants the words and claps)*

A chant can provide a backpiece for a rhyme. For example 'Tick Tock' is a chant, which can be whispered by a group of children as a solo performer recites the poem Hickory Dickory Dock. A support assistant could help the chanting group by keeping the rhythm with a chinese woodblock or other unpitched instrument.

Extension activities could include making up your own chants e.g. 'one banana, two bananas . . .'

Multiple voices

Rounds are an instance of chanting, which even young children can master. Short poems such as

> *There she goes*
> *There she goes*
> *All dressed up in her Sunday clothes*
>
> ANON

can be performed as a round for three performers, each taking one line and performing it three times - one child starting a line after the previous child and so on.

Chain gangs

NLS:

Year 2 Term 3
T11 to use humorous verse as a structure for children to write their own
S4 to read aloud with intonation and expression

PNS:
Speaking, Listening, Learning no. 20

Chain poems, where the children invent verses by substituting their own words into a pattern of rhyme and rhythm, can engage children in thinking creatively. For example:

Rhubarb Ted

> *I knew a funny little man*
> *His name was Rhubarb Ted*
> *They called him that because he wore rhubarb on his head.*
>
> ANNE O'CONNOR

was introduced to reception and Year 1 pupils who practised inventing their own verses:

I knew a funny little man
His name was cabbage Ted
They called him that because he wore
Cabbage on his head.

so that the poem could be presented during the plenary as a final performance.

A performance plan:

- tell children of the poem *My Brother Bert* by Ted Hughes and write '*My brother Bert has a mouse in his shirt*' on flip chart – investigate what makes this an interesting line (rhyme, rhythm, alliteration, humour);
- model writing the next line with the changed form of address
  Your brother Bert has a mouse in his shirt?
- demonstrate using two pupils performing a line each, how this could form the beginning of a chain poem;
- model writing the next two lines
  Well.........my Aunty Mabel drinks Carling Black Label
  Your Aunty Mabel drinks Carling Black Label?
  Well....
- rehearse with four pupils the beginning of the chain. Suggest other examples e.g. *My cousin Freddy is never ready*
  and ask for pupils' suggestions;
- organise pairs of children to compose two more lines and practise performing in independent time;
- support children in plenary to perform the whole chain. The alternate lines, which form a refrain, can be performed as a question or an exclamation, depending upon the facial expression, body language, and intonation.

When the children are confident in remembering the words, they can add a little movement to convince the audience of their role. For example hands on hips, staring incredulously, closing eyes in disbelief, conspiratorially whispering '*Well my Aunty Mabel...*' See page 39 for development ideas.

Chorus lines

NLS:
Year 2 Term 2 T10
to comment on and recognise when reading aloud of a poem makes sense and is effective;
S4 to read aloud with intonation and expression

Choral speaking is sometimes thought of as the preserve of the elocution teacher or something about which girl guides were enthusiastic in the 1950s, but in fact it is great fun as it teaches poetry in a powerful way, provides a purposeful listening context, and can build confidence in young performers. Initially children need to hear the melody and mood of a poem and engage with what the poet is trying to say, even though it may take many readings before they feel they reach a full understanding.

By marking up scripts and annotating them with children's names the teacher can demonstrate skimming, scanning and close reading. Children then use these skills in order to find their speaking part and follow the performance.

A performance plan:

This approach will exploit the eerie atmospheric tale of *Alone in the Grange* by Gregory Harrison (see page 27):

- read the poem to the children in a dramatic way, emphasising the wonderful sounds, rhythms and patterns. The twin-lined stanzas provide excellent opportunities for a varied use of voice – the hushed *Soft Soft* contrasts dramatically with *Black Black*, for example, which can be spat out;

- show children either an enlarged copy of the poem or an OHT. Read again and invite the children to join in the choruses to engage them in the mood of the poem;

- read two lines at a time and ask which children who would like to practise them for the final performance. Hold mini auditions inviting volunteers to perform selected lines. Ask children to comment constructively on others' performances. The aim is not to prove that one child is better than another – it is to encourage them to discuss their options and make creative choices. This they will need to do independently when they collaborate to prepare future poems;

- independent time can give the children time to try out dramatic techniques – experimenting with facial expressions and body language – an imaginary pair of spectacles made with thumb and forefinger for the line *peers with his dark eye*, for example. Practise, practise, practise, until the children can perform confidently without a script. Encourage pupils to work with a critical friend who thinks carefully about identifying strengths, which could include gestures, actions, mimes, voice quality etc. Pupils can draw upon previous teacher modelling of this process and should be able to present the same poem in different ways – building up a repertoire of approaches.

- in the plenary present a polished practice performance with the opportunity for taping or taking photos for display with the text.

Choral readings and group work will be easier for children if they have photocopies of poems, preferably laminated, so that text highlighters can be used to mark up scripts.

Adding movement and inserting dialogue

Movement allows children to get inside a poem and move around within it but there is a journey which children have to make before they can take part confidently in a production such as *The Lady of Shalott* described in chapter one. Teachers can support pupils in this journey by movement and drama work but many may be frightened that it is a specialist area in which they have no expertise. There are many simple ways in which movement can support performance work, however, which do not require special provision such as a hall or studio. The techniques described here can be achieved quite simply by using part of the classroom space. A poetry circle made by children sitting on the floor can make a natural forum for children to use as they perform their poems. In this way children are very aware of

the audience which surrounds them and they can use eye contact or even pointing to people to involve an audience in the poem.

Simply standing from a sitting position to recite a particular line can be effective. For example in the poem *One potato . . .* children can stand when they say their line and then the poem can ripple back down the line of performers so that the last performer says the first line and sits down.

A performance plan:

Michael Rosen's poem *Busy Day* lends itself to movement on the beat (see page 28):

- standing in a circle, at *pop in* the children do a feet-together jump towards the circle centre, and out again on *pop out*;
- *Pop over the road* is a left-hand jump, *pop out for a walk* a right hand jump.
- *Pop in for a talk* they hop to face an adjoining partner and use both hands to simulate speaking;
- *Pop down to the shop* hop to partner on other side and simulate buying;
- *can't stop, got to pop* is said in stillness then *pop where? pop what?* is said as children subside to sit on heels,
- then, slow rising and arms raising on slow saying of *w-e-l-l, I'-v-e g-o-t t-o*
- and the hopping starts again on *pop in* and poem and action continues.

Very soon children will want to move beyond simple movement sequences. In the case of *Busy Day*, this could be achieved by injecting snatches of dialogue, inserting, in keeping with the phrasing and timing of the poem, a choral *Hello!* after *pop in* and *Goodbye* after *pop out*, for example. *Pop over the road* could be followed by the 'vroooom' of a car passing, *pop out for a walk* to sounds of walking on gravel, for instance. In this way the poem serves as a starting point for a movement/word development that gives room to the children's ability to create. The poem therefore goes:

> *Pop in* (jump in)
> *(Hello!)*
> *pop out* (jump out)
> *(Goodbye!)*
> *pop over the road* (jump left)
> *(Vroom!)*
> *pop out for a walk* (jump right)
> *(Crunch, crunch)*
> *pop in for a talk* (hop to partner, chatter chatter with hands)
> *pop down to the shop* (hop to other partner)
> *(Bread please)*

can't stop (stillness)

got to pop (stillness)

got to pop?

pop where? (Going down)

pop what? (Sit on heels)

w-e-l-l (rising)

I'-v-e g-o-t t-o (rising)

Adding movement can support progression and engagement. As children gain in confidence they experiment with their own movement. Claire and Ben aged four decided that for the poem

Who's that tickling my back said the wall?

It's me said the caterpillar

I'm learning to crawl.

they would say the poem twice, taking it in turn to be the caterpillar who speaks his part as he crawls on the floor. This kind of experimentation will require more space and could be practised in the independent time of the literacy hour. Simple props such as hats, cloaks or masks can support children in working in role.

Drama

See pages 11 and

Some simple drama techniques can help performer and audience focus more closely on what is happening.

Still photographs are an effective way to freeze the moment as if caught unaware by a hidden camera. A group of Year 2 pupils came to the line *supposing she had caught nits in my head* from the poem *The School Nurse* by Ahlberg, and paused open mouthed as if registering their alarm to a hidden camera privy to their innermost thoughts. There is silence during the moment which in itself commands attention.

Statues can work well, when children make a tableau of still figures. If this happens at the beginning of a performance the audience can walk around and begin to wonder … The moment the figures move the performance begins – the silence can continue for a few moments as an effective way of commanding attention.

Using musical instruments

Instruments can be used effectively in many ways, for instance:
- to echo the syllabic structure the traditional skipping chant *Salt, mustard, vinegar pepper* can be performed with four unpitched instruments, with each instrument playing the syllables of one word. This can be done in an arrangement where the chant is played with instruments before the words are chanted. Simple scores can help children follow the sequence;

- to introduce sound effects. The rhyme *Hickory Dickory Dock*, for example, could use a xylophone for the mouse running up and down the clock, a metallophone for the Westminster chimes as an introduction to the poem, or the tick tock of the chinese woodblock as a background;
- unpitched instruments which keep the beat or emphasise certain beats e.g. **Pease** (tambourine) *Pudding hot,* **Pease** *Pudding cold,* **Pease** *pudding in the pot, Nine days old;*
- simple accompaniment of songs and rhymes using pitched instruments.

Unpitched instruments are especially suitable for very young children and would help them to respond with enjoyment, concentrating on rhythm and beat.

Poetry shows

As children develop as performers they should be able to spend more time planning and rehearsing their own work. This may mean that the structure of the literacy hour needs to be flexible. In Year 2 Term 3, for example, the objective T6 *to read, respond imaginatively and recommend and collect examples of humorous story extracts and poems* could mean that there is a very short shared time when the task is introduced and children then spend most of the hour finding poems, practising their presentation for an extended plenary. Alternatively, the plenary could be held over until the end of the next session so that children have time to practise and compare their work. The role of the teacher in this would be to provide suitable material and act as critical friend for work in progress. Director-pupils may have the tasks of putting together a final presentation – publishing a programme, for instance.

See pages 11 and 17

Mouth Open, Story Jump Out

I tell you me secret
You let it out
But I don't care
If the world hear
Shout it out

Mouth open
Story jump out
Mouth open
Story jump out

Beside the story I tell you wasn't even true
So you can shout till you're blue
So BOOOOOOOOOOOOOO

Mouth open
Story jump out
Mouth open
Story jump out
Mouth open
Story jump out

JOHN AGARD

See page 15

The Jumblies

I
They went to sea in a Sieve, they did,
  In a Sieve they went to sea:
In spite of all their friends could say,
On a winter's morn, on a stormy day,
  In a Sieve they went to sea!
And when the Sieve turned round and round,
And every one cried, 'You'll all be drowned!'
They called aloud, 'Our Sieve ain't big,
But we don't care a button! We don't care a fig!
  In a Sieve we'll go to sea!'
    Far and few, far and few,
      Are the lands where the Jumblies live;
      Their heads are green, and their hands are blue,
      And they went to sea in a Sieve.

II
They sailed away in a Sieve, they did,
In a Sieve they sailed so fast,
  With only a beautiful pea-green veil
Tied with a riband by way of a sail,
  To a small tobacco-pipe mast;
And every one said, who saw them go,
'O won't they be soon upset, you know!
For the sky is dark, and the voyage is long,
And happen what may, it's extremely wrong
  In a Sieve to sail so fast!'
    Far and few, far and few,
      Are the lands where the Jumblies live;
      Their heads are green, and their hands are blue,
      And they went to sea in a Sieve.

III
The water it soon came in, it did,
  The water it soon came in;
So to keep them dry, they wrapped their feet
In a pinky paper all folded neat,
  And they fastened it down with a pin.
And they passed the night in a crockery-jar,
And each of them said, 'How wise we are!
Though the sky be dark, and the voyage be long,
Yet we never can think we were rash or wrong,
  While round in our Sieve we spin!'
    Far and few, far and few,
      Are the lands where the Jumblies live;
      Their heads are green, and their hands are blue,
      And they went to sea in a Sieve.

IV   *And all night long they sailed away;*
            And when the sun went down,
          They whistled and warbled a moony song
          To the echoing sound of a coppery gong,
            In the shade of the mountains brown.
          'O Timballo! How happy we are,
          When we live in a Sieve and a crockery-jar,
          And all night long in the moonlight pale,
          We sail away with a pea-green sail,
            In the shade of the mountains brown!'
              Far and few, far and few,
                Are the lands where the Jumblies live;
                Their heads are green, and their hands are blue,
                And they went to sea in a Sieve.

V   *They sailed to the Western Sea, they did,*
            To a land all covered with trees,
          And they bought an Owl, and a useful Cart,
          And a pound of Rice, and a Cranberry Tart,
            And a hive of silvery Bees.
          And they bought a Pig, and some green Jack-daws,
          And a lovely Monkey with lollipop paws,
          And forty bottles of Ring-Bo-Ree,
            And no end of Stilton Cheese.
              Far and few, far and few,
                Are the lands where the Jumblies live;
                Their heads are green, and their hands are blue,
                And they went to sea in a Sieve.

VI   *And in twenty years they all came back,*
            In twenty years or more,
          And every one said, 'How tall they've grown!
          For they've been to the Lakes, and the Torrible Zone,
            And the hills of the Chankly Bore!'
          And they drank their health, and gave them a feast
          Of dumplings made of beautiful yeast;
          And every one said, 'If we only live,
          We too will go to sea in a Sieve,––
            To the hills of the Chankly Bore!'
              Far and few, far and few,
                Are the lands where the Jumblies live;
                Their heads are green, and their hands are blue,
                And they went to sea in a Sieve.

EDWARD LEAR

See page 20

Alone in the Grange

Strange,
Strange,
Is the little old man
Who lives in the Grange.
Old,
Old,
And they say that he keeps
A box full of gold.
Bowed,
Bowed,
Is his thin little back
That once was so proud.
Soft,
Soft,
Are his steps as he climbs
The stairs to the loft.
Black,
Black,
Is the shuttered house.
Does he sleep on a sack?
They say he does magic,
That he can cast spells,
That he prowls round the garden
Listening for bells;
That he watches for strangers
Hates every soul,
And peers with his dark eye
Through the key hole.
I wonder, I wonder,
As I lie in my bed,
Whether he sleeps with his hat on his head?
Is he really a magician
With altar of stone,
Or a lonely old gentleman
Left on his own?

GREGORY HARRISON

See page 21

Busy Day

Pop in
pop out
pop over the road
pop out for a walk
pop in for a talk
pop down to the shop
can't stop
got to pop

got to pop?

pop where?
pop what?

well
I've got to
pop round
pop up
pop in to town
pop out and see
pop in for tea
pop down to the shop
can't stop
got to pop

got to pop?

pop where?
pop what?

well
I've got to
pop in
pop out
pop over the road
pop out for a walk
pop in for a talk...

MICHAEL ROSEN

CHAPTER 2

Moving on

*'It brings poetry alive – that's what I like about it –
otherwise poetry is flat on the page'*
Debbie, Year 5 and 6 teacher

As children become more confident they need challenging in their poetry performance work but what does progression involve?

A wider range of poems

During the last twenty years schools have echoed to the chants, rhythms and rhymes of the new wave poets: Michael Rosen, Gareth Owen, Allan Ahlberg, Brian Patten. The list is a long one and this informal and child-friendly strain of poetry has raised the profile of poetry in school. Poets such as Benjamin Zephaniah and John Agard have introduced poems from a variety of other cultures and traditions. These genres are often children's first choice.

Progressing to a wider variety of texts is important and prescribed by the National Curriculum and National Literacy Strategy. Genres detailed in both documents are particularly appropriate for performance. They include raps, narrative poetry, classical poetry, including Shakespeare songs and limericks. Raps are cool, and children may discover these for themselves but are less likely to seek out classic work. This has important implications for the teacher.

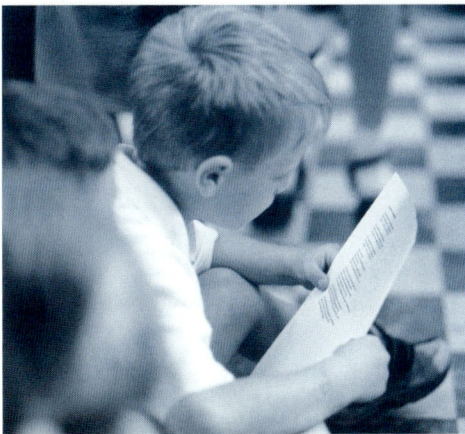

A wider range of music techniques

Poetry performance can be enhanced through the use of unpitched instruments. This can become more sophisticated and the children's musical and manipulative skills develop. Early on, contributions are often limited to being on the beat, but half and double time can be used with effect and pitched instruments played by class members introduced. Their use may

not be too advanced to begin with, e.g. a glockenspiel playing to the rhythm of the words, chimebars to provide an interval between verses as performers rearrange themselves. Later, individual skills in a class can be employed, e.g. a flute used on just five fluttery notes to accompany a sea poem, a simple piano tune to introduce and end a poem's performance. Later, ways in which the music and words interact can be explored, allowing a fusion of forms. Poems can be transformed into songs either in their entirety, or by keeping the verses spoken, but with the whole class singing the chorus. The orchestration of chosen musical contributions is an important task which children grow into. Co-ordinating a woodblock rhythm with the voices of five children making sound effects for the train, together with the recorders and glockenspiel interacting with the words, is a very sophisticated task. The challenge is to employ the developing musical skills of the class members without loading the poem and its performance with unnecessary and unhelpful clutter.

A wider range of drama techniques

Young children use forms of dramatic play quite naturally and, if the drama is suitably clear and structured, can become deeply involved. With very young children, teachers will have to provide scaffolding for this to take place. It is not possible, for example, for most five-year olds to work in unsupervised subgroups upon a theme from a poem. With good structure and appropriate introduction to drama techniques, however, this should be possible with older primary children. There is, of course, strong support for drama work in the Primary National Strategy (*Speaking, Listening, Learning, working with children in Key Stages 1 & 2*, DfES 2003), and the published leaflet *Drama – making it work in the classroom* makes a handy poster. Find the web reference for downloading it on page 73.

Drama involves a complex blend of intellectual, physical and emotional responses. Learning is not a passive activity, but involves the child in finding meaning through speaking and moving in imagined environments. It is this principle of the blending of body, mind and feelings that makes drama such a successful learning medium. As with any art form, children need to be introduced to the symbolic language that is drama if they are to use it successfully. We cannot expect children to progress in their abilities to make music unless they learn more about rhythm, tone, instruments and, eventually, notation. So it is in drama where we must teach those techniques that allow the child to explore and represent the imagined world effectively. A limited range of approaches is suggested here in the expectation that, having tried them, teachers will not only choose to use those with which they are most comfortable, but will invent variations and new approaches. There are a range of books and courses that provide more information on using drama in the primary school; a few are shown on page 73 at the end of the book.

The key to using drama is to find that which is *dramatic* within the poem. Without this essential 'dramatic power' simple visual representation can be superfluous to the poem's effectiveness and, in some cases, can devalue it. The awful truth to bear in mind is that hordes of children in masks and costume can act as a lead weight on a poem's messages if the attempt at dramatic representation is not truly dramatic.

'Finding what is dramatic' often requires active exploration through the drama, although as children become more experienced they are able to 'read' a poem in ways that allow them to predict which images and sequences might make the best drama. It is important to be selective as a poem may contain a great range of images; understanding the hierarchy of images and meanings is a necessary way of digesting the poem's structure and performance potential.

The ways described here in which children can create imaginary physical worlds are essential as the constant search for realistic costume, props and scenery is often unnecessary and can severely hamper the development of the children's performance of the poem. Whilst judicious use of props and costume can assist, the ill-fitting crown and the bendy cardboard sword can be a serious obstruction and distraction. We, and especially children, can create better king's gear in our imaginations.

Active exploration

The child should come to see drama as a useful approach to exploring, clarifying and communicating a poem's meaning. A limited amount of time is usually required to set the parameters of such exploration, but as soon as is possible, the children should be on their feet and exploring the poem through action – thinking through the medium of drama. The first stage should be challenging, but limited in difficulty and duration. The teacher might say,

'Can you make a statue of the troll when he sees that his pot of gold has disappeared?' or

'Let's make a group statue of the Pied Piper leading the children into the mountain.'

These images could be developed through 'thought tracking' (a process where, when touched on the shoulder, characters speak what they are thinking or saying at the moment which the statue depicts) into mini improvisations.

Children are very good at thinking through the drama, for it is only when they are trying to capture a perceived meaning within the medium that they also have new, often more sophisticated thoughts on what the meaning might *be*. There is therefore an exciting symbiosis between content and form – the meaning and the drama. A typical example is:

Child 1: 'So we come in as the children and the Pied Piper starts to dance, and we see him and go to see what's happening.'
(They try it, but half way through a child says. . .)

Child 2: 'No, I think we are playing in the street and we hear the sound of his pipe and we start to dance without realising it and as he comes around the corner, we are already under his spell.'
(They try it and agree that this is better. Another child says...)

Child 3: 'And Rachel and Manuel are our parents and they can't understand what we are doing, but when they come to grab us, they can't move quickly because of the magic music.'

The ideas occur in the act of *doing*, so it is restrictive of children's development of the performance if the teacher expects that they will work everything out before 'getting up to do it.' It is also important that this process is called 'devising through improvisation' or 'exploration' as the term 'rehearsal' carries the inference that the work to be performed is already fixed and the children just need to practise.

The teacher's role is to set the parameters within which the devising described above can happen, to organise and support the work and to challenge children to review what they are doing and make decisions about its effectiveness and where to go next. Creativity works best when the exploration is bounded by well-chosen limitations. She must also provide the resources, including suitable space, for effective drama work to happen. If children are working in groups, she must scan constantly the groups to assess their progress and be ready to inject new impetus when required. A simple metaphor for this is that the teacher energises the activity as they might wind up a clockwork toy. Just as the toy slows down when the spring needs rewinding, when the poetry / drama task in hand begins to wane, the teacher needs to step in and re-energise the work.

The teacher is also instrumental in bringing the class together to allow ideas to be shared. Opportunities for public performance can be acquired by encouraging children not just to tell about their work, but also to show what they are developing through the medium of drama. In most cases this should be seen as 'work in progress' and, following its sharing with the rest of the class, the group doing it should first be asked 'what do you like about what you have done?' then 'what would you like to work on more if you had time?' before asking the same questions of those watching. No one should be forced to 'share' their work if they are not ready to do so, and the social atmosphere must be very positive to allow unfettered contributions.

The teacher, aided by children who are not immediately involved in the drama, must also act as an 'audience eye' constantly questioning, as the performance date approaches, whether the performance will communicate clearly.

Physical theatre

Children are wonderful improvisers. They are used in their own play activities to adapting environments and the objects they contain to make imaginative worlds. Physical theatre allows them to use their bodies to create the physical surroundings in performance. The king's throne can be made with children's bodies, the dark wood through which the lambs pass, or the houses that contain the three little pigs can all be made by the arrangement of limbs and torsos. Once children understand how this approach works, they become very resourceful in its use. See the *Pied Piper* performance plan (page 45) for examples.

Mime

Simply, mime is the ability of an actor to use an environment and artefacts within it *as though they were present*. Once the imaginary physical environment is created by the group, due respect must be given to it, for example the positioning of the cauldron, its size and shape. This shared understanding is most often achieved by being part of or watching the drama rather than listening to explanations. Children can choose which aspects of the physical environment they will create, then practise miming their use. See *The Village Shop* performance plan on page 43 for examples.

White mime

In white mime, the actor draws the shape of the imaginary object in the air accompanied by suitable sounds. So, in *The Pied Piper* (see page 45), for example, a mayor's hat might be drawn in outline with both forefingers, using vocal sounds as each section is drawn. The splendid feather is drawn similarly and then the rich jewels are 'punched' on to it with jabs of the forefinger and plosive vocal sounds. In the early stages the children or teacher/narrator can also use words, so *The Mayor wore a wonderful hat* – (shape drawn) – *with a splendid feather* – (shape drawn) – *and ringed with the most beautiful jewels – peet! peet! peet!* (child performer stabs in jewels.) The mayor then puts on the hat and behaves accordingly.

This kind of theatre is useful in two ways: it releases children from the need to have the 'right' costume to be able to tell the story and it allows the participants and audience to make a much better, exotic hat in their imagination than can ever be achieved in reality. The environment of performance can also be created in white mime. A window can be drawn with forefingers in the air, with accompanying sound, and then the actor who has drawn it can, using mime, open it and look out.

The attraction of creating imaginary physical environments, costumes and props is that they can be changed and developed at will. As described above, the process of developing poetry performance is a dynamic one in which each episode of work brings new realisations about a poem's meanings and how they might be explored and captured in the drama. Imaginary environments and objects can easily be changed, whilst actual, physical ones made in good faith may at best become redundant, or at worst hold back the development of the work. An example might be that in week one the children decide that the animals in the poem are dogs, so the teacher spends many hours making dog masks ready for the next session, during which the children discover that the animals they see in the poem are not dogs, but zebras!

Stylised and naturalistic forms

Naturalistic drama is drama which represents things as they really are. This places emphasis on real time, place and characterisation. Thus a poem that has embedded in it the making of a gingerbread man will require extended naturalistic dramatic representation as the flour is weighed, the butter, sugar and water added, the ingredients mixed, rolled and stamped out, then the cooking .... etc. In stylised form, children can jump as individual ingredients into a 'bowl' speaking their name 'flour!' 'eggs' etc then 'mix' their bodies for a few seconds before unravelling in a line of gingerbread men. Some one says '200 degrees centigrade!' and the gingerbread men stiffen whilst making a 'sizzling' noise. All done in fifteen seconds!

Children will be limited greatly if naturalistic drama is the only form to which they have access. Stylised drama allows all kinds of wonderful things to happen. A whole day – or a lifetime – can be condensed into a matter of seconds. Human beings can transform into monsters, inanimate objects come alive. One approach to stylised work is to challenge children to represent a naturalistic scene of, say, two minutes into a stylised one of fifteen seconds. This can be achieved by selecting the key images and words from the naturalistic scene, then arranging them into a satisfying stylised representation. Being able to manipulate the dramatic medium is such ways constitutes an important aspect of progression.

Costume

Because the range of characters created by children is potentially enormous it is impossible to store all costumes in appropriate sizes that may be needed. If children begin to accept that they can only really progress with the development of a character or scene once the correct costume is obtained, it will seriously hamper the work. It is much better to have a range of simple tabards of different colours and sizes, together with lengths of coloured material. These items are adaptable to many kinds of usage (the affixing of cut-out symbols to the tabards, for example) and can be supplemented by a particular costume item if required. Again, the principle applies that children can imagine much grander robes than the teacher can possibly find.

Masks

With face paint, it is possible to transform a child's face. This is easily achieved and removed. Simple masks can be made from cardboard and can be enhanced by the addition of appendages such as hair and tendrils. More sophisticated masks can be made from *papier maché* or by building

1 A full stick mask. Made from *papier maché*, but simple ones can be made from flat card.

2 A basic half-mask which allows the character to speak. Made from *papier maché* with an elastic head strap.

3 A woolly hat enables a change of character.

4 Victorian card character masks. These are very simple to use and children can make others like them. A set of these can be obtained from Pollock's Toy Museum, Covent Garden. See them on the web at http://www.tao 2000net.f9.co.uk/ pollocks/masks.htm

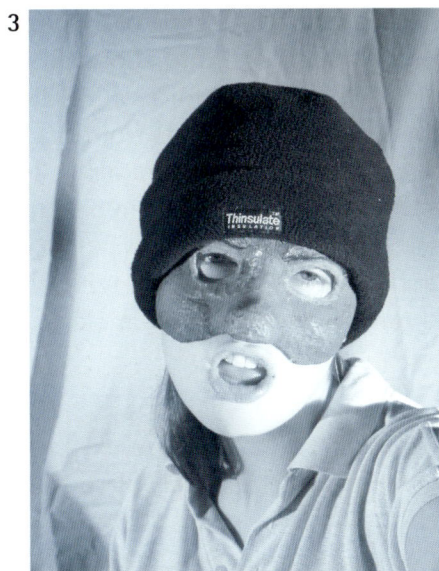

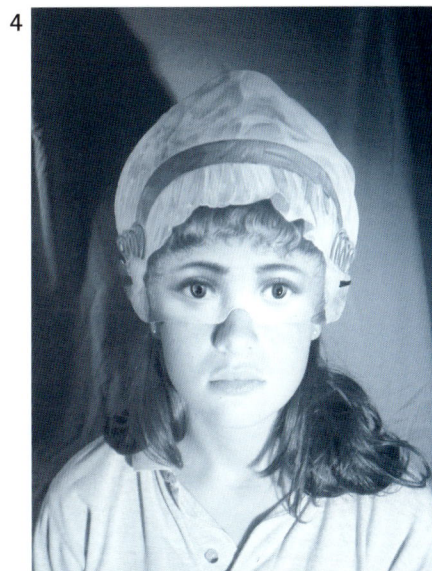

5 See 4.

6 A full wolf mask. Inside this *papier maché* exterior there is a helmet mask: the basic shape is made on a balloon with *papier maché* and *papier maché* additions are imposed once the main mask is dry.

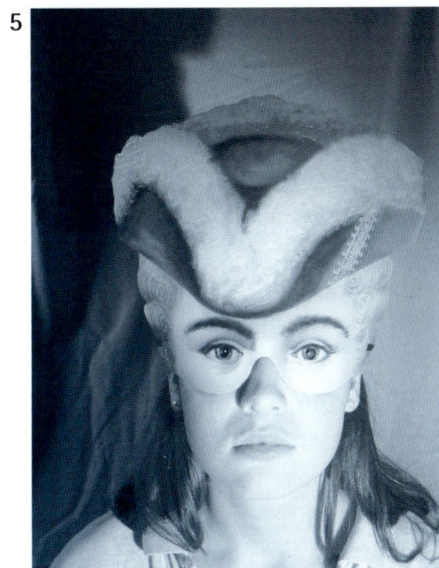

additional features onto a bought neutral mask. Good fitting is required if the wearer is to feel comfortable and not constantly 'fiddle' with the mask. Small bands of foam can be used inside the mask at forehead and cheeks to keep the mask clear of eyes and nose. Half masks (ending above the mouth) are essential if wearers are required to speak and be heard clearly.

Puppets

Shy children can often feel safer projecting a poem through a puppet. Marionettes are almost always too difficult to manipulate, but glove or rod puppets can be effective and simply made. Effective first-stage puppets can also be created around a wooden spoon with the face being painted on the bowl. Glove puppets can be created on a sock. Rod puppets are best constructed around a given frame containing a central dowel-rod body with shoulder strut that carries articulated arms to which the rods are connected. A face is created on card that can be fixed to the rod protruding above the shoulders, and card hands glued to the ends of the arms (see diagram).

A big box of material scraps is useful to allow children choice of puppet clothing. Silver and gold card is helpful for making crowns, wands etc. A booth can be created from high-jump stands from the sports cupboard with a cloth thrown over the bar. This arrangement also allows for use by different age groups as the height of the bar can be adjusted. Simple scenery can be cut from card and coloured and held in place on the top edge of the booth. A stage crew can be responsible for changing this appropriately. There is great potential for progression in the making and use of puppets.

Shadow work

A simple screen of white material stretched onto a frame (say 3m x 2m) can be used with a light behind it to allow the children to experiment with creating shadows by placing themselves between the light and the screen. At first, they will want just to use their hands to create shapes, but once they are introduced to the varied effects that can be achieved - making things bigger by advancing to the light source, for example - they will quickly explore its potential. Theatre lantern gel can be placed in front of the light to create different effects.

Use of overhead projector

To create backgrounds for poetry performance, children can draw directly onto acetates which can then be projected onto a light-coloured wall or, to avoid children's bodies casting shadows, back projected onto the white screen mentioned above (see diagram on next page). Alternatively, children's paintings can be colour photocopied onto acetates. Examples of OHP use are given in the performance notes on *Green Man, Blue Man* (page 44). Progression is achieved through finding imaginative ways to enhance the performance through such image creation.

1   Wire rings with twisted wire joints pushed into holes.

2   Rod puppet body with card face. Children can experiment with the face until satisfied with the features.

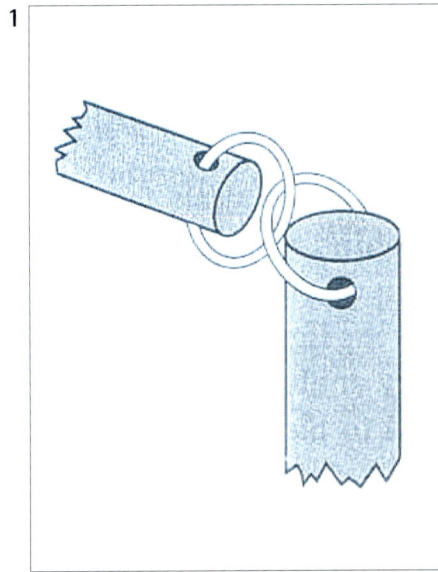

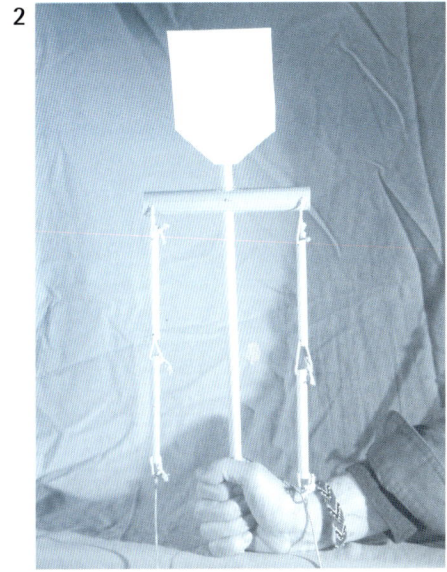

3   A nurse rod puppet. The puppet is supported by one hand and the arms are manipulated with the other. Dowel rod body, arms jointed with string through holes. Face of card. Clothes stapled and glued in place.

4   African woman rod puppet.

5   A hand puppet supported on index finger (head) and fore and third fingers (arms). Small card tubes are positioned to take the fingers. Head of wood, polystyrene or card. Material glued and stapled in place.

6   A stick puppet: a block of wood or polystyrene supported on and manipulated by a length of dowel rod. Card and material can be glued to the basic head shape and the whole painted.

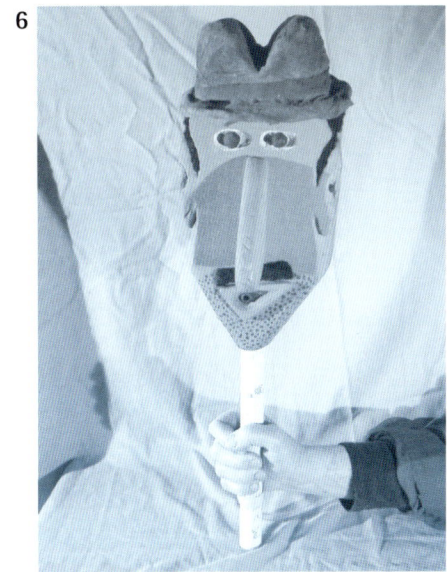

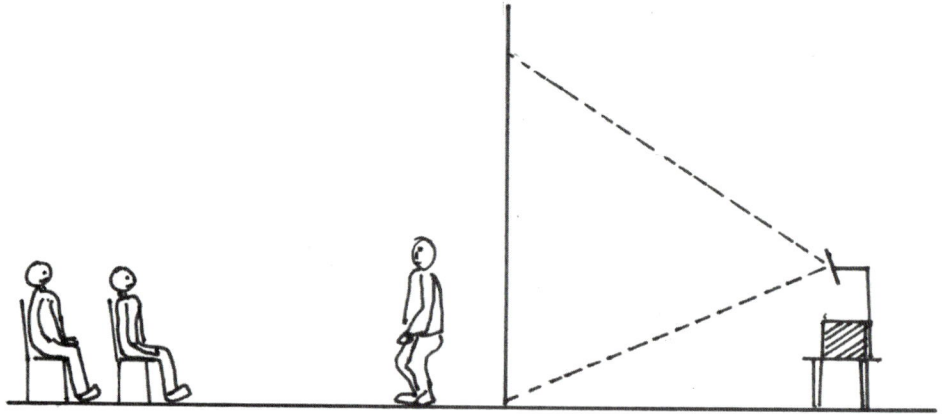

Staging

The use of simple rostra can help in creating a more varied environment for exploration of poems and poetry performance. Ideally, these should be safe and light enough for children to manipulate them unaided. Uprights can be fixed to the rostra to form supports for further scenery, e.g. banners, a doorway or a stylised tree. The creation of more challenging environments for poetry performance is one element of progression to be encouraged in the work. Children can make more sophisticated choices about moving in and out, over and through the environment they have created.

Lighting and sound

Magic environments can be created if a blackout can be achieved and simple lighting is available. A directional table lamp with a domestic rotary dimmer switch between it and the power supply can suffice for simple work, but two spotlights with a slider dimmer allow more sophisticated effects. Light is most useful for editing work – allowing sequences to begin and end with dramatic effect as images appear and fade. A single lighting stand with a t-bar would allow both spots to be mounted safely. Tape cables to the bottom of the stand and the floor to avoid accidents.

The use of recorded music can provide atmospheres for poetry performance. Children can also lay down their own soundtracks to suit their work by recording voice, music and sound effects onto a cassette tape or mini disc recorder. Choosing and customising the sound used is an important element of progression. Most hi-fi systems have a facility for plugging in a microphone which allows voice amplification and the creation of vocal sound effects. The latter are very useful as they can be adapted as the performance plans develop. The microphone can be useful for creating effects or boosting the volume of some elements in the poetry performance (e.g. the giant's voice.)

CHAPTER 3

Poetry performances – sample plans and notes

The following approaches spring from our work in schools. They demonstrate some of the techniques described earlier in the book. The activities indicated are suggestions only and teachers should feel free to adapt them. Some of the most exciting work comes through exploring the inter-relationship of the rhythms of words, sounds and movements. Much of this can only be discovered through practical exploration. It is important that the teacher finds positive frameworks in which such exploration can occur. It is essential that the performance techniques supplement and amplify the power and rhythmic coherence of the poem. As presented, the six plans and indicated objectives roughly progress through year groups – Reception to Year 6 – but there are absolutely no hard and fast rules about using them in this order.

A class discussion could take place at the end of the poetry performance process in which the children reflect on their performance in relation to its effectiveness, form and content, including comparisons to other dramas they have created or seen. This could be followed by a written task, for example where they, as evaluators, make notes on a grid which has space for their comments next to specific areas presented for focus by the teacher, e.g. certain characterisations, use of space, movement, choruses, use of props etc.

PLAN ONE **The Family**

NLS:
RY T10 to re-read and recite stories and rhymes with predictable and repeated patterns objectives.

Yr 2 Term 3 T 6 to read and respond imaginatively, recommend and collect examples of humorous stories, extracts, poems; S1 to

read text aloud with intonation and expression appropriate to grammar and punctuation.
Yr 1 Term 3 T 9 to read a variety of poems on similar themes e.g. families, school food; S3 to read familiar texts aloud with pace and expression appropriate to grammar.

The following is a poetry show which was performed by pupils from Reception, Year 1 and Year 2. The children had made their own version of *My Brother Bert* as described on p.19 and used this as a chorus throughout the show. The other poems used are *Going through the old photos* by Michael Rosen, *My Dad, Your Dad* by Kit Wright, *My Sister Laura* by Spike Milligan, and *My Sister Jane*, by Ted Hughes.

The children were seated in a poetry ring into which performers move to recite.

Children welcome audience and each introduces themself with a rhyme they have composed:

All children in turn	*(e.g. Hello I'm Jennifer King and I wear a ring.)*
First performer	*My brother Bert's got a mouse in his shirt*
Second performer	*Your Brother Bert's got a mouse in his shirt!* *Well, My Aunty Mabel drinks Carling Black Label . . .*
Third performer	*When we go over* *to my granddad's* *he falls asleep.* *While he's asleep* *he snores.*
Fourth performer (seated)	*(snoring noises)*
Third performer	*When he wakes up* *He says,*

Fourth performer	*Did I snore?*
	        Did I snore?
	        Did I snore?

All	*No you didn't snore*
Third performer	*Why do we lie to him?*

(**Going through the old photos** by **Michael Rosen**)

Fifth performer	*Your Aunty Mabel drinks Carling Black Label* *Well My Aunty Nelly's got a pain in her belly*
Sixth performer	*(sitting looking at photos with seventh performer)* *Who's that?*
Seventh performer	*That's your Aunty Mabel* *And that's me* *under the table*
Sixth performer	*Who's that?*
Seventh performer	*That's Uncle Billy.*
Sixth performer	*Who's that?*
Seventh performer	*Me being silly.*
Sixth performer	*Who's that* *Licking a lolly?*
Seventh performer	*I'm not sure* *But I think its Polly*
Sixth performer	*Who's that* *Behind the tree?*
Seventh performer	*I don't know* *I can't see.* *Could be you* *Could be me.*

Sixth performer	*Who's that?*
Seventh performer	*Baby Joe.*
Sixth performer	*Who's that?*
Seventh performer	*I don't know.*
Sixth performer	*Who's that standing on his head?*
Seventh performer	*Turn it round.*
	It's Uncle Ted.

(Going through the old photos by Michael Rosen)

Eighth performer	*Your Aunty Nelly's got a pain in her belly* *Well my Uncle Fred lives in a shed*
Ninth performer	*Cousin Nell* *Married a frogman* *In the hope* *That one day he would turn into a handsome prince.*
Tenth performer	*(Yes but) Instead he turned into* *A sewage pipe*
Eleventh performer	*near Gravesend*
Tenth performer	*And was never seen again.*

(Cousin Nell by Roger Mc Gough)

Twelfth performer	*Your Uncle Fred lives in a shed* *Well my Cousin Jim is very, very dim*
Thirteenth performer	*My dad's fatter than your dad,* *Yes, my dad's fatter than yours:* *If he eats any more he won't fit in the house* *He'll have to live out of doors.*
Fourteenth performer	*Yes but my dad's balder than your dad* *My dad's balder OK* *He's only got two hairs left on his head* *And both are turning grey.*
Fifteenth performer	*Ah, but my dad's thicker than your dad,* *My Dad's thicker alright.* *He has to look at his watch to see if it's noon* *Or the middle of the night.*
Sixteenth performer	*Yes but my dad's more boring than your dad* *If he ever starts counting sheep* *When he can't get to sleep at night, he finds* *It's the sheep that go to sleep.*
	But my dad doesn't mind your dad
Fifteenth performer	*Mine quite likes yours too*
All	*I suppose they don't always think much of us!*
Sixteenth performer	*That's true I suppose that's true.*

(My Dad, Your Dad by Kit Wright)

Seventeenth performer

My sister Laura's bigger than me
And lifts me up quite easily (Sister Laura lifts her)
I can't lift her (trying) I've tried and tried
She must have something heavy inside.

(My Sister Laura by Spike Milligan)

Eighteenth performer

Your cousin Jim is very, very dim
You should see my cousin Pat, she's enormously fat.

All chant

Sisters sisters sisters . . .

Nineteenth
– twenty-second
performers (*as a round*)

If only I hadn't had sisters
How much more romantic I'd be
But my sisters were such little blisters
That all old women are sisters to me

(Anon)

Twenty-third performer

And I say nothing – no, not a word
About our Jane. Haven't you heard?
She's a bird, (one voice) a bird, (two voices) a bird, (three) a bird (four)

Four voices chorus

Oh it never would do to let folks know
My (our) sister's nothing but a great big crow

Twenty-fourth
performer

Each day (we daren't send her to school)
She pulls on stockings of thick blue wool
To make her pin crow legs look right,
Then fits a wig of curls on tight,
And dark spectacles a huge pair
To cover her very crowy stare

Four voices chorus

Oh it never would do to let folks know
My (our) sister's nothing but a great big crow

Twenty-fifth performer

When visitors come she sits upright
(with her wings and her tail tucked out of sight)
They think her queer but extremely polite.
Then when the visitors have gone she whips out her wig and with her wig on
Whirls through the house at the height of your head –
Duck, duck or she'll knock you dead

Four voices chorus

Oh it never would do to let folks know
My (our) sister's nothing but a great big crow

Twenty-sixth performer

At meal times whatever she sees she'll stab it –
Because she's a crow and that's a crow's habit
My mother says 'Jane your manners please!'
Then she'll sit quietly on the cheese,
Or play the piano nicely by dancing on the keys –

Four voices chorus

Oh it never would do to let folks know
My (our) sister's nothing but a great big crow

(My Sister Jane by Ted Hughes)

(All blow a variety of wind instruments to create windy sound)

Twenty-seventh
performer

Through every nook and every cranny
The wind blew in on poor old Granny
Around her knees, into each ear
(and up her nose as well I fear)

All through the night the wind grew worse
It nearly made the vicar curse
The top had fallen off the steeple
Just missing him and other people

It blew on man; it blew on beast
It blew on nun; it blew on priest
It blew the wig off Aunty Fanny
But most of all it blew on Granny.

(Granny by Spike Milligan)

PLAN TWO *The Village Shop* **by Sarah Hopkins and her class**

NLS:

Year 3 Term 3 T7
*to select, prepare, read
aloud and recite by heart
poetry that plays with
language or entertains.*

*PNS Speaking,
Listening, learning no.
36*

For the complete text of the poem, see page 49.

As a variant to published poetry, this poem was written by a teacher and children in a village school. Each section (two stanzas) constitutes a statement by a shopkeeper and a response from a customer.

Each stanza contains the names of different customers, shopkeepers and products. These can be adapted to suit local circumstances. The class can be split into seven groups, each working on a separate section. Each group uses stylised drama to represent the production of the food or items the customer requires. The performance of each section is achieved by using two children from another group to act as shopkeeper and customer whilst, at the end of the verse, the group which had been working on it enacts the production. In the first section, for example, the group shows the planting of the wheat, its growth and harvesting, grinding and baking, then the cow grazing, being milked, the cheese-making process, and its cutting, wrapping and delivery to the shop by lorry. This must be done speedily (hence the use of stylised drama which does not rely on 'real time') whilst maintaining the momentum of the poem.

Full sound effects are provided vocally by the group members themselves (lots of fun to be had here!) Percussion sound can be provided by others. Customer and shopkeeper freeze whilst the product enactment takes place then, as the 'producers' of the products melt away, the shopkeeper says something like

> *There we are Mr Braithwaite, some bread and beautiful cheddar.*

The customer says

> *Thank you Mrs Morris, see you tomorrow*

and leaves. The performance involves the whole class, many of them in multiple roles.

The performance can be preceded and ended, and the verses linked by a collective chorus:

> *The people in the shop go chatter chatter, chatter,*
> *Chatter, chatter, chatter, chatter, chatter, chatter,*
> *The people in the shop go chatter, chatter, chatter,*
> *All day long.*

Chorus:
> *Chitter chatter, chitter chatter, chitter chatter, chitter chatter,*
> *chitter chatter, chitter chatter, chitter chatter CHIT!*

The chorus can be sung to the tune and rhythm of *The Wheels on the Bus* (http://www.bbc.co.uk/cbeebies/tweenies/songtime/songs/t/thewheelsonthebusfull.shtml) and can be augmented by the use of unpitched percussion instruments.

PLAN THREE   *Green Man, Blue Man* **by Charles Causley**

NLS:

Year 4 Term 2 T7
To identify different patterns of rhyme and verse in poetry, e.g. choruses, rhyming couplets, alternate line rhymes and to read these aloud effectively.

For the complete text of the poem, see page 50.

The images to be found in this poem are realised through dramatic representation, in this case with the help of an overhead projector.

A simple approach with this poem would be to split the class into groups representing the colours green, blue, grey and purple. Each child wears clothing approximating to the verse colour. Everyone makes a simple mask of an appropriate colour. The action for each verse is negotiated with the children. In the first verse, for example, this might be:

Green group stands facing a light-coloured wall or a suspended white sheet. Overhead projector (OHP) is switched on to frame and illuminate them. Rest of class speaks:

> *As I was walking through Guildhall Square*
> *I smiled to see a green man there,*

As this is being spoken, the green men turn to face out.

> *But when I saw him coming near*

Green group advances on watchers to sound of suitable percussion and/or whispering, to final climax of last part of line 'coming near, coming near, coming near, coming near!'

> *My heart was filled with nameless fear.*

Green group makes menacing movements towards watchers and freezes – watchers let out short scream. OHP off.

(Groups' change-over is covered by live music or chanting of key words or phrases from the poem *Green man tat-a-tat, blue man, bah-bah-bah*).

Green group quietly exits and sits. Blue group (suitably dressed and masked) takes position. OHP on with acetate decorated with 'raindrops':

> *As I was walking through Madford Lane*
> *A blue man stood there in the rain*

As this is spoken some blue men hold out hands to feel rain, others bring hands up over heads in attempt to stay dry. All lower heads on chests. Rain sound simulated with rain stick or other percussion and or children's chant of *Plip plop, plip plop . . .*

> *I asked him in by my front door*

Half the blue men simulate doors and turn through 90 degrees with creaking sound. The others stand upright, look ahead and put out hands as if to shake that of the person inviting them in.

> *For I'd seen a blue man before.*

OHP faded by sliding a piece of card over lens as blue group advances on watchers and watchers say 'Before, before; before, before'. . .

Grey and purple groups are developed in similar ways. The last verse could be worked by using theatre lantern gel of the four colours to produce a collage of colours and covering the OHP platter with this to produce a melange of colours. This could be done by cutting the gel into small squares and fitting them onto an A4 sheet of clear acetate. Some children from each of the four groups move in the light, whilst the rest speak the verse.

> *But when the night falls dark and fell*
> *How, O how, am I to tell,*
> *Grey man, green man, purple, blue,*
> *Which is which, is which of you?*

Everyone repeats the last line in whispers of decreasing volume whilst the OHP is adjusted out of focus until the colours blur and merge. Children speak last whisper and freeze – five-second silence and stillness, then OHP off.

PLAN FOUR   *The Pied Piper of Hamelin* by Robert Browning

NLS:

Year 5 Term 3 T4 to read, rehearse and modify performance of poetry; T6 to explore the challenge and appeal of older literature.

PNS Speaking, Listening, Learning no. 57

(For the complete text of the poem, see page 51)

It is possible to draw out quite complex narrative images from a ballad poem, in this case to bring alive Robert Browning's poem 'The Pied Piper of Hamelin'.

Introduce white mime to the children (see page 33). Use it to represent Hamelin Town itself. As the first verse is narrated, children take up positions that represent the houses and the town hall and its clock. The houses can be shown by upright bodies and arms making a triangle around the head to show the roof structure.

The town hall can be similarly made with the child on a stool to make the building higher. Other children can make it more grand – flying buttresses etc. A ticking forearm and a swinging other arm for the pendulum can symbolise the clock which strikes when the 'hand' reaches vertical. More complex clocks can be made with other children representing

cogs and spindles. A pre-strike chime or tune can be built in. The river can be represented with a long, billowing cloth or by two townspeople who punt past the buildings whilst discussing the rat problem.

At the end of the first verse, the children who are the houses transform themselves into the residents of those buildings, opening the windows (after first establishing them with white mime) to talk to each other about the rats. Each speaks a snippet – just enough to establish the idea in a watcher's imagination. The whole group then freezes and transforms suddenly into squeaking rats on the speaking of 'Rats!' at the start of verse two.

After the initial action and squeaking, the group freezes again and sub-groups represent sections of the rat action suggested in the second verse: biting babies, licking ladles, eating cheese etc.

The mayor creates his own hat and gown and chain of office in white mime (see page 33), assuming a deeper role as each is donned, finally sticking out his stomach and patting it in contentment. Verse XI can be developed through statue work with the figures emerging from and disap-pearing into stone.

Once the early exercises of this kind are complete, and children catch the spirit of how drama works in this context, they often show a great ability to invent within the dramatic medium.

PLAN FIVE *The Lady of Shalott* by Alfred Lord Tennyson

NLS:

Year 5 Term 2 T5
to perform poems in a
variety of ways.

PNS Speaking,
Listening, Learning no.
54

For the complete text of the poem, see page 55.
Because this is a long ballad poem the children should be introduced to it through a well-prepared reading by the teacher. This should be followed by some discussion of meaning-although this should not and cannot be exhaust-ive. The exploration of the poem through drama is the chief way in which

the meaning of the poem is discovered. Children think through the drama.

It is very important that the children become aware of pace as the way in which the tempo changes reflects the meaning – slow and dreamy for the scene setting, dramatic and dynamic for the entrance of Sir Lancelot, menacing and mysterious for the slow descent in death. Pace is also important in mirroring the changing phases of the river as it glides, rushes and tumbles by turn.

You will not need all of the verses, simply the ones which carry the story line, i.e. one, five and six. These three verses work well juxtaposed as they are very different in pace and tempo. There are four verses which describe Sir Lancelot and the first one may suffice as, importantly, it intro-duces a dramatic change of tempo. The tense can be changed into the present for the scene where The Lady is weaving her web as this draws the audience more intimately into the scene.

The characters of The Lady and Lancelot can be played by more than one child. Two Sir Lancelots can work very well as the Knight is in two very different moods: he comes joyfully into Camelot but becomes disturbed and pensive. Other pupils can be townspeople, reapers, troops of damsels glad, acting as a backdrop to whoever is narrating the story.

It is recommended that the narration be shared by several children. If the class is used to drama work, they can devise the scenes suggested by the poem, and this responsibility can be shared among sub-groups after the story is divided up. There is opportunity for some choral work, e.g. 'The Lady of Shallot', is a repeated final line of some stanzas, or all narrators might recite the dramatic verse where the Lady sees the knight, for example. Particular sections can be spoken by the characters themselves – especially where direct speech is indicated. The Lady herself can speak 'the curse is come upon me . . .' for example.

Props and costume can be very simple: a head dress and gown made from old net curtains for The Lady and a stool for her to sit on, a cloak, shield and helmet for Sir Lancelot (avoid cheap plastic props that may look comical).

Linda, whose Year 6 class enacted this poem comments: *'I learnt a lot from this production. I'd been very nervous as I'm not a drama teacher or a teacher of Key stage two and the children had not done much drama. However what I hadn't realised was that the poem itself dictated the production. The children were transformed as they worked with total involvement. Their own understanding of themselves enabled them to cast the parts – Alice, for example, as the Lady of Shallott was rather a shy girl who moved beautifully in an ethereal sort of way, almost abstracting herself from the scene so that the few words she actually spoke were even more dramatic. Using two pupils as Sir Lancelot worked really well as the knight is in two very different moods: he comes joyfully into Camelot but becomes disturbed and pensive All the children understood the plot – not from my explanation but from engagement, from the inside out and from each other as they demonstrated their own response. Unusual words such as 'casement' presented no problems – I didn't bother explaining them. The production enthused not just the children but also their families and the wider school community and the university students to whom they performed.'*

PLAN SIX   *The Secret* by Gareth Owen

NLS:

Year 6 Term 3 T4
to comment critically on
the overall impact of a
poem, showing how
language and theme have
been developed.

PNS Speaking,
Listening, Learning no.
67

For the complete text of the poem, see page 57.

Once children are used to working on poems in this way and are comfortable in using drama techniques that expand the poem rather than repeat or limit its imagery, they should be able to make decisions about the structure and performance of a poem. 'The Secret' by Gareth Owen could be used with older primary children who have some experience of creative group work in drama and perhaps have worked on poems under teacher guidance.

The poem is episodic with a journey at its core. Drama could be used most effectively at the end of each verse. If purely mime, the action could be covered by the creative use of the last line of each verse. Thus, the words at the end of verse 2:

> *Remember, no one must know*
> *The secret you've learned today, today*
> *The secret you've learned today.*

could be sung in a haunting way – maybe making it into a round. It could be used following each verse as the drama action takes place, changing after the last verse to its last lines:

> *Your secret is safe with me, with me*
> *Your secret is safe with me.*

The class can be split into groups, each covering a different verse. In the enactment, those subgroups can call on the whole class if necessary to realise their vision for a particular verse.

A combination of physical theatre techniques could be used to represent the imagery of the poem. Several children could make the well and its voice, whilst the journey through the 'secret wood' and the 'soft breeze' that blows through the ' briar and the rose' plus the beach and its gulls are easily explored through the children using their bodies and voices and musical instruments. The secret's growth can be symbolised by the group representing this concept physically and the valley leading to the well can be represented by bodies which part as the poet makes the journey through it. The children then transform into the well and its voice. There is potential for very moving resonances of the secret between the teller and the well. The whole poem has potential for choral delivery. Once the individual groups have experimented with and shaped their work to their satisfaction, they could be invited to share their work with the rest of the class prior to a 'master plan' being developed for the whole poem.

A suitable closing image could be the whole class whispering 'safe with me' as they close in from representations of trees, valley and people to completely cover the well and seal in its 'secret.'

See note on page 39 about evaluating the performance.

The Village Shop
BY SARAH HOPKINS AND CLASS

1. *Hello Mr Braithwaite*
   Fancy seeing you
   How're you doing down at the farm?
   And what can I do for you?

   Well Mrs Morris
   I need some bread and cheese
   I'd like to take some brown bread
   And a lump of cheddar please.

2. *Hello Mrs Hopkins*
   Fancy seeing you
   How're you doing down at the school
   And what can I do for you?

   Well Mr Dingle
   I need some bread and cake
   I'd like to take some lollies
   And a loaf for me to bake

3. *Hello Mr Breadman*
   Fancy seeing you
   How're you doing at the bakery
   And what can I do for you?

   Well Mrs Carter
   I need some milk and cheese
   I'd like to take some biscuits
   And a bar of chocolate please.

4. *Hello Mrs Gardner*
   Fancy seeing you
   How're you doing down at the Theme
   Park
   And what can I do for you?

   Well Mrs Salter
   I need some ham and eggs
   I'd like to take some sweeties
   And a little bag of pegs.

5. *Hello Mr Rusty*
   Fancy seeing you
   How're you doing down at the dump
   And what can I do for you?

   Well Mrs Plum
   I need some fish and chips
   I'd like to take some bacon
   And some grapes without their pips.

6. *Hello Molly Braithwaite*
   Fancy seeing you
   How're you doing down at the playschool
   And what can I do for you?

   Well Mr Wheatcroft
   I need some crisps and peas
   I'd like to take some milk shake
   And a comic if you please

7. *Hello PC Thompson*
   Fancy seeing you
   How're you doing down at the station
   And what can I do for you?

   Well Mrs Tucker
   I need some exotic teas
   I'd like some tasty toffee
   And a Cornish pasty please.

Green Man, Blue Man

BY CHARLES CAUSELY

As I was walking through Guildhall Square
I smiled to see a green man there,
But when I saw him coming near
My heart was filled with nameless fear.

As I was walking through Madford Lane
A blue man stood there in the rain
I asked him in by my front door,
For I'd seen a blue man before.

As I was walking through Landlake Wood
A grey man in the forest stood,
But when he turned and said, 'Good Day'
I shook my head and ran away.

As I was walking by Church Stile
A purple man spoke there a while.
I spoke to him because, you see,
A purple man once lived by me.

But when the night falls dark and fell
How, O how, am I to tell,
Grey man, green man, purple, blue,
Which is which, is which of you?

The Pied Piper of Hamelin
BY ROBERT BROWNNG

I

Hamelin town's in Brunswick,
By famous Hanover city;
The river Weser, deep and wide,
Washes its wall on the southern side
A pleasanter spot you never spied;
But when begins my ditty,
Almost five hundred years ago,
To see the townsfolk suffer so
From vermin, what a pity!

II

Rats!
They fought the dogs and killed the cats,
And bit the babies in the cradles,
And ate the cheeses out of the vats,
And licked the soup from the cook's own ladles.
Split open the kegs of salted sprats,
Made nests inside men's Sunday hats,
And even spoiled the women's chats
By drowning their speaking
With shrieking and squeaking
In fifty different sharps and flats.

III

At last the people in a body
To the town hall came flocking:
"'Tis clear," cried they, "our mayor's a noddy;
And as for our corporation-shocking
To think we buy gowns lined with ermine
For dolts that can't or won't determine
What's best to rid us of our vermin!
Rouse up, sirs! Give your brains a racking
To find the remedy we're lacking,
Or, sure as fate, we'll send you packing!"
At this the mayor and corporation
Quaked with a mighty consternation.

IV

An hour they sat in council;
At length the mayor broke silence
"For a guilder I'd my ermine gown sell;
I wish I were a mile hence!
It's easy to bid one rack one's brain-

I'm sure my poor head aches again,
I've scratched it so, and all in vain.
Oh for a trap, a trap, a trap!"
Just as he said this, what should hap
At the chamber door but a gentle tap!
"Bless us," cried the mayor, "what's that?"
(With the corporation as he sat
Looking little though wondrous fat;
Nor brighter was his eye, nor moister
Than a too-long-opened oyster,
Save when at noon his paunch grew mutinous
For a plate of turtle green and glutinous),
"Only a scraping of shoes on the mat
Anything like the sound of a rat
Slakes my heart go pit-a-pat!"

V

"Come in!" – the mayor cried, looking bigger:
And in did come the strangest figure!
His queer long coat from heel to head
Was half of yellow and half of red,
And he himself was tall and thin,
With sharp blue eyes, each like a pin,
And light loose hair, yet swarthy skin,
No tuft on cheek nor beard on chin,
But lips where smiles went out and in;
There was no guessing his kith and kin:
And nobody could enough admire
The tall man and his quaint attire.
Quoth one: "It's as my great-grandsire,
Starting up at the trump of doom's tone,
Had walked this way from his painted
tombstone!"

VI

He advanced to the council table:
And, "Please your honors," said he, "I'm able,
By means of a secret charm, to draw
All creatures living beneath the sun,
That creep or swim or fly or run,
After me so as you never saw!
And I chiefly use my charm
On creatures that do people harm,
The mole and toad and newt and viper;

And people call me the Pied Piper."
(And here they noticed round his neck
A scarf of red and yellow stripe,
To match with his coat of the selfsame check;
And at the scarf's end hung a pipe;
And his fingers, they noticed, were ever straying
As if impatient to be playing
Upon this pipe, as low it dangled
Over his vesture so old-fangled.)
"Yet," said he, "poor piper as I am,
In Tartary I freed the Cham,
Last June, from his huge swarms of gnats;
I eased in Asia the Nizam
Of a monstrous brood of vampire bats:
And as for what your brain bewilders,
If I can rid your town of rats
Will you give me a thousand guilders?"
"One? fifty thousand!" – was the exclamation
Of the astonished mayor and corporation.

VII

Into the street the piper stepped
Smiling first a little smile,
As if he knew what magic slept
In his quiet pipe the while;
Then, like a musical adept,
To blow the pipe his lips he wrinkled,
And green and blue his sharp eyes twinkled,
Like a candle flame where salt is sprinkled;
And ere three shrill notes the pipe uttered,
You heard as if an army muttered;
And the muttering grew to a grumbling;
And the grumbling grew to a mighty rumbling;
And out of the houses the rats came tumbling.
Great rats, small rats, lean rats, brawny rats,
Brown rats, black rats, grey rats, tawny rats,
Grave old plodders, gay young friskers,
Fathers, mothers, uncles, cousins,
Cocking tails and pricking whiskers,
Families by tens and dozens,
Brothers, sisters, husbands, wives –
Followed the piper for their lives.
From street to street he piped advancing,
And step for step they followed dancing,
Until they came to the river Weser,
Wherein all plunged and perished!
– Save one who, stout as Julius Caesar,
Swam across and lived to carry
To rat-land home his commentary:

Which was, "At the first shrill notes of the pipe,
I heard a sound as of scraping tripe,
And putting apples, wondrous ripe,
Into a cider-press's gripe:
And a moving away of pickle-tub-boards,
And a leaving ajar of conserve-cupboards,
And a drawing the corks of train-oil-flasks,
And a breaking the hoops of butter-casks:
And it seemed as if a voice
(Sweeter far than by harp or by psaltery
Is breathed) called out, 'Oh rats, rejoice!
The world is grown to one vast drysaltery!
So munch on, crunch on, take your nunchion,
Breakfast, supper, dinner, luncheon!'
And just as a bulky sugar-puncheon,
All ready staved, like a great sun shone
Glorious scarce an inch before me,
Just as methought it said, 'Come, bore me!'
– I found the Weser rolling o'er me."

VIII

You should have heard the Hamelin people
Ringing the bells till they rocked the steeple.
"Go, cried the mayor, "and get long poles,
Poke out the nests and block up the holes!
Consult with carpenters and builders,
And leave in our town not even a trace
Of the rats!" when suddenly, up the face
Of the piper perked in the market place,
With a "First, if you please, my thousand
guilders!"

IX

A thousand guilders! The mayor looked blue;
So did the corporation too.
To pay this sum to a wandering fellow
With a gypsy coat of red and yellow!
"Beside," quoth the mayor with a knowing wink.
"Our business was done at the river's brink;
We saw with our eyes the vermin sink,
And what's dead can't come to life, I think.
So, friend, we're not the folks to shrink
From the duty of giving you something for drink,
And a matter of money to put in your poke;
But as for the guilders, what we spoke
Of them, as you very well know, was in joke.
Beside, our losses have made us thrifty.
A thousand guilders! Come, take fifty!"

X

The piper's face fell, and he cried,
"No trifling! I can't wait. Beside,
I've promised to visit by dinner time
Bagdat, and accept the prime
Of the head cook's pottage, all he's rich in,
For having left, in the caliph's kitchen,
Of a nest of scorpions no survivor:
With him I proved no bargain driver,
With you, don't think I'll bate a stiver!
And folks who put me in a passion
May find me pipe after another fashion."

XI

"How?" cried the mayor, "d'ye think I brook
Being worse treated than a cook?
Insulted by a lazy ribald
With idle pipe and vesture piebald?
You threaten us, fellow? Do your worst,
Blow your pipe there till you burst!"

XII

Once more he stepped into the street
And to his lips again
Laid his long pipe of smooth straight cane;
And ere he blew three notes (such sweet
Soft notes as yet musician's cunning
Never gave the enraptured air)
There was a rustling that seemed like a bustling
Of merry crowds justling at pitching and
hustling,
Small feet were pattering, wooden shoes
clattering
Little hands clapping and little tongues
chattering,
And, like fowls in a farmyard when barley is
scattering
Out came the children running.
All the little boys and girls,
With rosy cheeks and flaxen curls,
And sparkling eyes and teeth like pearls,
Tripping and skipping, ran merrily after
The wonderful music with shouting and
laughter.

XIII

The mayor was dumb, and the council stood
As if they were changed into blocks of wood,

Unable to move a step, or cry
To the children merrily skipping by,
– Could only follow with the eye
That joyous crowd at the piper's back.
But how the mayor was on the rack,
And the wretched council's bosoms beat,
As the piper turned from the High Street
To where the Weser rolled its waters
Right in the way of their sons and daughters
However he turned from South to West,
And to Koppelberg Hill his steps addressed,
And after him the children pressed;
Great was the joy in every breast.
"He never can cross that mighty top!
He's forced to let the piping drop,
And we shall see our children stop!"
When, lo, as they reached the mountain side,
A wonderous portal opened wide,
As if a cavern was suddenly hollowed;
And the piper advanced and the children
followed,
And when all were in to the very last,
The door in the mountain side shut fast.
Did I say, all? No! One was lame,
And could not dance the whole of the way;
And in after years, if you would blame
His sadness, he was used to say, –
"It's dull in our town since my playmates left!
I can't forget that I'm bereft
Of all the pleasant sights they see,
Which the piper also promised me.
For he led us, he said, to a joyous land,
Joining the town and just at hand,
Where waters gushed and fruit trees grew,
And flowers put forth a fairer hue,
And everything was strange and new;
The sparrows were brighter than peacocks here,
And their dogs outrun our fallow deer,
And honeybees had lost their stings,
And horses were born with eagles' wings:
And just as I became assured
My lame foot would be speedily cured,
The music stopped and I stood still,
And found myself outside the hill,
Left alone against my will,
To go now limping as before,
And never hear of that country more!"

XIV

Also, alas, for Hamelin!
There came into many a burgher's pate
A text which says that heaven's gate
Opes to the rich at as easy rate
As the needle's eye takes a camel in!
The mayor sent East, West, North, and South,
To offer the piper, by word of mouth,
Whatever it was men's lot to find him,
Silver and gold to his heart's content,
If he'd only return the way he went,
And bring the children behind him.
But when they saw 'twas a lost endeavor,
And piper and dancers were gone forever,
They made a decree that lawyers never
Should think their records dated duly
If, after the day of the month and year,
These words did not as well appear,

  "And so long after what happened here
  On the twenty-second of July,
  Thirteen hundred and seventy-six:"

And the better in memory to fix
The place of the children's last retreat,
They called it the Pied Piper's Street,
Where any one playing on pipe or tabor
Was sure for the future to lose his labor.

Nor suffered they hostelry or tavern
To shock with mirth a street so solemn;
But opposite the place of the cavern
They wrote the story on a column,
And on the great church window painted
The same, to make the world acquainted
How their children were stolen away,
And there it stands to this very day.
And I must not omit to say
That in Transylvania there's a tribe
Of alien people who ascribe
The outlandish ways and dress
On which their neighbors lay such stress,
To their fathers and mothers having risen
Out of some subterranean prison
Into which they were trepanned
Long time ago in a mighty band
Out of Hamelin town in Brunswick land,
But how or why, they don't understand.

XV

So, Willy, let me and you be wipers
Of scores out with all men – especially pipers!
And whether they pipe us FROM rats or FROM mice,
If we've promised them aught, let us keep our promise.

The Lady of Shalott

BY ALFRED, LORD TENNYSON

PART I

ON either side the river lie
Long fields of barley and of rye,
That clothe the wold and meet the sky;
And thro' the field the road runs by
      To many-tower'd Camelot;
And up and down the people go,
Gazing where the lilies blow
Round an island there below,
      The island of Shalott.

Willows whiten, aspens quiver,
Little breezes dusk and shiver
Thro' the wave that runs for ever
By the island in the river
      Flowing down to Camelot.
Four grey walls, and four grey towers,
Overlook a space of flowers,
And the silent isle imbowers
      The Lady of Shalott.

By the margin, willow-veil'd,
Slide the heavy barges trail'd
By slow horses; and unhail'd
The shallop flitteth silken-sail'd
      Skimming down to Camelot:
But who hath seen her wave her hand?
Or at the casement seen her stand?
Or is she known in all the land,
      The Lady of Shalott?

Only reapers, reaping early
In among the bearded barley,
Hear a song that echoes cheerly
From the river winding clearly,
      Down to tower'd Camelot:
And by the moon the reaper weary,
Piling sheaves in uplands airy,
Listening, whispers 'Tis the fairy
      Lady of Shalott.'

PART II

There she weaves by night and day
A magic web with colours gay.
She has heard a whisper say,
A curse is on her if she stay

To look down to Camelot.
She knows not what the curse may be,
And so she weaveth steadily,
And little other care hath she,
      The Lady of Shalott.

And moving thro' a mirror clear
That hangs before her all the year,
Shadows of the world appear.
There she sees the highway near
      Winding down to Camelot:
There the river eddy whirls,
And there the surly village-churls,
And the red cloaks of market girls,
      Pass onward from Shalott.

Sometimes a troop of damsels glad,
An abbot on an ambling pad,
Sometimes a curly shepherd-lad,
Or long-hair'd page in crimson clad,
      Goes by to tower'd Camelot;
And sometimes thro' the mirror blue
The knights come riding two and two:
She hath no loyal knight and true,
      The Lady of Shalott.

But in her web she still delights
To weave the mirror's magic sights,
For often thro' the silent nights
A funeral, with plumes and lights,
      And music, went to Camelot:
Or when the moon was overhead,
Came two young lovers lately wed;
'I am half sick of shadows,' said
      The Lady of Shalott.

PART III

A bow-shot from her bower-eaves,
He rode between the barley-sheaves,
The sun came dazzling thro' the leaves,
And flamed upon the brazen greaves
      Of bold Sir Lancelot.
A red-cross knight for ever kneel'd
To a lady in his shield,
That sparkled on the yellow field,
      Beside remote Shalott.

The gemmy bridle glitter'd free,
Like to some branch of stars we see
Hung in the golden Galaxy.
The bridle bells rang merrily
          As he rode down to Camelot:
And from his blazon'd baldric slung
A mighty silver bugle hung,
And as he rode his armour rung,
          Beside remote Shalott.

All in the blue unclouded weather
Thick-jewell'd shone the saddle-leather,
The helmet and the helmet-feather
Burn'd like one burning flame together,
          As he rode down to Camelot.
As often thro' the purple night,
Below the starry clusters bright,
Some bearded meteor, trailing light,
          Moves over still Shalott.

His broad clear brow in sunlight glow'd;
On burnish'd hooves his war-horse trode;
From underneath his helmet flow'd
His coal-black curls as on he rode,
          As he rode down to Camelot.
From the bank and from the river
He flash'd into the crystal mirror,
'Tirra lirra,' by the river
          Sang Sir Lancelot.

She left the web, she left the loom,
She made three paces thro' the room,
She saw the water-lily bloom,
She saw the helmet and the plume,
          She look'd down to Camelot.
Out flew the web and floated wide;
The mirror crack'd from side to side;
'The curse is come upon me!' cried
          The Lady of Shalott.

PART IV

In the stormy east-wind straining,
The pale yellow woods were waning,
The broad stream in his banks complaining,
Heavily the low sky raining
          Over tower'd Camelot;
Down she came and found a boat
Beneath a willow left afloat,
And round about the prow she wrote
          The Lady of Shalott.

And down the river's dim expanse –
Like some bold seer in a trance,
Seeing all his own mischance –
With a glassy countenance
          Did she look to Camelot.
And at the closing of the day
She loosed the chain, and down she lay;
The broad stream bore her far away,
          The Lady of Shalott.

Lying, robed in snowy white
That loosely flew to left and right –
The leaves upon her falling light –
Thro' the noises of the night
          She floated down to Camelot:
And as the boat-head wound along
The willowy hills and fields among,
They heard her singing her last song,
          The Lady of Shalott.

Heard a carol, mournful, holy,
Chanted loudly, chanted lowly,
Till her blood was frozen slowly,
And her eyes were darken'd wholly,
          Turn'd to tower'd Camelot;
For ere she reach'd upon the tide
The first house by the water-side,
Singing in her song she died,
          The Lady of Shalott.

Under tower and balcony,
By garden-wall and gallery,
A gleaming shape she floated by,
Dead-pale between the houses high,
          Silent into Camelot.
Out upon the wharfs they came,
Knight and burgher, lord and dame,
And round the prow they read her name,
          The Lady of Shalott.

Who is this? and what is here?
And in the lighted palace near
Died the sound of royal cheer;
And they cross'd themselves for fear,
          All the knights at Camelot:
But Lancelot mused a little space;
He said, 'She has a lovely face;
God in His mercy lend her grace,
          The Lady of Shalott.'

The Secret
BY GARETH OWEN

Down a secret path
Through a secret wood
By the side of a secret sea,
I creep on tiptoe
To a place I know
That no one can find except me, except me
That no one can find except me.

And the soft breeze that blows
Through the briar and the rose
That I pass along my way
Seems to whisper low,
"Remember, no one must know
The secret you've learned today, today
The secret you've learned today."

Beside that beach
Where the herring gulls screech
And the long cream breakers roll,
The voice of the sea
Whispers softly to me,
"You must not tell a soul, a soul
You must not tell a soul."

But the secret I know
Seems to grow and grow
Until it weighs me down like a load,
If I don't tell someone
Before very long
I'm sure I'm going to explode, explode
I know that I'm going to explode.

Up a path from the beach
I finally reach
A valley deep and wide,
And it's here that I tell
To an old stone well
The secret I've kept hidden inside, inside
The secret I've kept hidden inside.

In that deep well's ear
Where no one will hear
I whisper secretly
And from miles away
Each word I say
Comes echoing back to me, to me
Comes echoing back to me.

And I make my well
Promise never to tell
The words whispered secretly,
And like a far-away bell
Tolls the voice of the well,
"Your secret is safe with me, with me
Your secret is safe with me."

CHAPTER 4

ICT and poetry performance

*'Increased capability in the use of ICT promotes initiative and
independent learning.'*
(DfEE 2000 The National Curriculum)

It is poetry week in a village primary school. In the playground a knot of
foundation pupils is working with their teacher on a school picnic table
trying to learn a chain poem. She is helping their concentration by
recording it a line at a time, each child contributing one line, and then
playing back the whole poem. Inside school some Year 1 and 2 pupils are
working independently with a tape recorder, taping and assessing their
performance. In years 3 and 4 children are taking digital photographs of a
performance in progress. In years 5 and 6 children are searching a web site
for poems to support their forthcoming poetry show. Information and
communication technology has an important role to play in supporting
young performers.

Cassette tape recorders

These can help pupils to review, modify and evaluate work as it progresses,
reviewing what they have done and talking about how they might change
it (NC KS1 PoS 4a and 4c). Young performers may find it difficult to learn
lines but learning and reciting a few at a time can help them memorise
large chunks of text. Children who are diffident in front of an audience are
often happy to work on recording and other technical tasks with the teacher
or other pupils.

Older children can make and edit tapes which can be played for a
variety of audiences, e.g. a series of tapes with a radio programme format
like Radio 4's *Poetry Please*. Tapes can then form part of the school's library
or resources kept in class. One class of foundation pupils we worked with
had a library of tapes in the wigwam which formed part of their play area.

Because of the availability of cassette tape recorders, it is possible to
provide groups with their own recording system. Each will need to work in
a space in which their recording is not interrupted by extraneous noise.

Mini disc recorders

The quality of recording on mini disc is potentially of much higher quality than that achieved on a tape recorder. Mini disc recordings can be made a track at a time, then reordered, deleted, edited and given names. It is possible to have flexible track access so, unlike using the cassette recorder, there is no problem with trying to find the correct place. Track access time is very quick, so if a pupil's input to a chain poem was track 6, once recorded, track 6 could be pressed for play back without the inconvenience of tape counters, or fast-forwarding or rewinding.

Most mini disc recorders will have a shuffle-play function. This enables a selection of tracks to be played back in a completely random order. Using this function it is possible to make a random 'poem generator'. Children could record lines of a poem and then the complete poem could be played back using the shuffle-play mode. Because of the random nature of the playback each hearing is reordered and different. Both mini disc and standard cassette tape recordings can be played into a computer using a 'line-in' jack and then transferred to compact disc for sharing or archiving.

Because of its recording sensitivity, a mini-disc is capable of producing an excellent sound reproduction of a poetry performance.

Mini disc tips can be found at:

http://www.minidisc.org/tips_index.html

CD ROMs

Children should gather information from a variety of sources (NC KS1 PoS 1a). There is a variety of CD ROMs to support children's listening skills and help them learn new poems, e.g. *Ridiculous Rhymes* by Sherston Software. The highly-recommended book *Rap it Up* by James Carter (see page 73) is packaged with a CD featuring performances by Valerie Bloom and Brian Moses, and backing tracks for pupils to use with their own performances.

Recordable CD ROMs allow children to engage with poetry in a much more interactive way. They can empower the child and help to give them control of their learning direction. They can also give the child instant feed back and offer prompts to encourage experimentation. Using a computer in this way children are much more likely to take risks and 'have a go'. CD ROMs can offer a safe, non-threatening and non-judgmental environment in which children can explore at their own pace. CD ROMs can be used to record video, stills and sound.

Top tips for using CD ROMs in Literacy can be found at:

http://curriculum.becta.org.uk/literacy/resources/cdromtips.html

Video recording

As the NC says, *children in KS2 need to be sensitive to the needs of audience and think carefully about the content and quality when communicating information (KS2 Pos 3b).* Videoing work in progress can support this process, improving children's critical facilities and *helping them evaluate how they and others have contributed to the overall effectiveness of performances* (KS 2 Pos EN 1 4d). Final performance videos can be used for display work around the school if they are left continually running.

Many digital still cameras have the ability to record short bursts of simple video. These can range in time from 15 seconds to a minute. In a classroom context this is often just the correct amount of time you may wish to use. The quality of the video is not as good as using a dedicated video camera. Sequences can be reviewed and judged on the spot by using the small screen on the back of the camera. The short sound bites of video can be transferred to a computer in the same way as still images. Once in the computer they can be edited into mini videos. The new version of the Windows (XP) operating system comes with editing software, *'Movie Maker'*, as standard. More sophisticated free software, AVID DV, is available at http://www.avid.com/freedv/. It is possible to come up with a finished result in a matter of minutes. These can be shared via the internet or written to a CDR (Recordable Compact Disc).

Older children can video suitable images, then marry these with the words of a poem dubbed onto selected images. An example is the videoing of shots of children's paintings with a poem being spoken over, with suitable music played softly in the background. Another could be created from outside shots of a river or sea with music and words dubbed over. There are obvious opportunities for progression in this area of the work through the production of scenarios, storyboards, purpose-made painted backgrounds or models and even animation.

Simple video editing software can be found at:
http://www.microsoft.com/windowsxp/using/moviemaker/default.mspx
http://www.ulead.co.uk/dps/runme.htm

The internet

In the planning stages there are many web sites which teachers and pupils can use to search for poems which are particularly suitable for performance. Publishers' web sites often give information and downloadable examples of poems. For performance, school websites can feature poems read aloud by children or video clips of performance.

The internet, therefore, offers the following advantages:
- it's an excellent form of publishing;
- children's work can be read anywhere in the world;
- work can be updated and adapted – it is a changing medium;
- children can manage their own content;
- work can be targeted at appropriate audience by using a password system;
- discussion groups and forums can help to redraft and refine good work and practice;
- there are unlimited resources for the class teachers;
- it is a medium for sharing good practice and ideas;

- it is a multimedia environment, work can include sound and video;
- performance can be augmented by displays of text.

Through the use of web cameras and video conferencing, it is possible for children to perform a poem for a remote audience and for them to receive performances originated elsewhere. Thus it is possible for children in England and Australia to work on the same poem, then share the outcomes.

Multimedia presentations

These can be a very effective way of shaping creative responses from children. PowerPoint presentations can feature children's drawings and voices to support the text. Longer ballad type poems can be published in a talking book format. Presentation software, such as PowerPoint, can enable the written word to spring to life. Subtle use of animations and graphics can greatly enhance and complement work. It is possible to embed video and sound files into a presentation. The rhyme and metre of poetry can be accentuated and made explicit by use of highlighted or animated text. This can help to give the children an enhanced understanding of form and structure. The children's own written work and drawings can be scanned, cropped, edited and enhanced by the use of multimedia tools. Once finished the work is ready to share and is easily redrafted or adapted.

Rats!
They fought the dogs and killed the cats,
And bit the babies in the cradles,
And ate the cheeses out of the vats,
And licked the soup from the cook's own ladles,

This is an example from Year 5 pupils who were working on performance of *The Pied Piper of Hamelin* by Robert Browning.

A PowerPoint tutorial can be found at:

http://www.actden.com and

http://training.peoriaud.k12.az.us/inoutclassms/content/ppt97/default.htm

Word processing

Highlighting texts to identify parts can be done on screen and programmes, posters and invitations can all be published to support performance.

Using a word processor enables the child to redraft and adapt work quickly and efficiently so that poems can be written or downloaded from the internet and then edited using key tools such as spellchecker and the thesaurus. Many word processors found in school have the ability to read text back to a child, providing a very valuable form of proof reading. Images can be scanned and inserted into text to provide a good source for attractive mini publications such as anthologies. Digital photographs taken during poetry shows can be used in this way to produce a lasting record of poetry performances. Children can also produce worksheets of chain poems, leaving suitable blank spaces for filling in by other classes.

Illustrated anthologies of poems can be produced, with the word processing and graphics being completed by pupils.

Resources to support use of ICT include:

Interactive Teaching, Communicative Teaching: ICT and Classroom Teaching by D. Cook and H. Finlayson, Open University Press 1999

ICT and literacy: information and communication technology, media, reading and writing by N. Gamble and N. Easingwood, Continuum 2001

Internet: The Impact on our Lives by I. Graham, Raintree Steck-Vaughn Publishers 2001

ICT in the Early Years by M. Hayes (Ed), Open University 2004

Teaching and Learning with ICT in the Primary School by M. Leask and J. Meadows, Routledge Falmer 2000

The school's guide to the INTERNET by P. McBride, Heinemann 1998

Computers and Language by M. Monteith (Ed), Intellect Books 1993

Opportunities for Information and Communication Technology in the Primary School by H. Smith, Trentham Books 1999

Web sites

BECTa (British Educational Communications and Technology Agency) (including links to NGfL and the VTC): **http://www.becta.org.uk**

ICTeachers (resources for teachers): **http://www.icteachers.co.uk**

Infant Explorer (Kent LEA literacy website): **http://www.naturegrid.org.uk/infant**

Virtual Teacher Centre (VTC): **http://vtc.ngfl.gov.uk**

CHAPTER 5

Extending the journey: publishing and other challenges

'They want to do more now. Some have started to bring poems into school and ask to read them to the class'
(Sarah, Year 5 teacher)

If children are to see poems as an integral part of life as opposed to 'special occasions' they must experience them in a variety of forms, styles and contexts. This chapter looks at a number of ways in which this might happen[1].

Web pages

It is now extremely straightforward to create a web page especially for poetry and accessed independently and through links from a school website. This can contain poems selected by pupils from their own and other poets' work. The website can carry comment by those who produced it and from those who access it. In this way an interactive site can be developed. The site can contain visuals too – illustrations related to poems which can comprise photographs (say of a local river to accompany a 'river' poem) or illustrations produced by students. Web-site advice on the web is too complex and jargon-ridden for children to cope with. Far better to seek the help of an IT literate parent and local authority expert on IT. Overleaf is some work done by eleven-year-olds in connection with *The Pied Piper of Hamelin*.

PowerPoint

These images were also included in a twenty-image PowerPoint presentation with the accompanying sound of children reading the poem. This can be accessed by children on a PC or can form an impressive presentation for projection onto a big screen through a data projector.

---

1   In relevant cases, teachers must be aware of issues of copyright when choosing to publish the work of established, modern poets. Guidance on copyright can be obtained at www.copyrightservice.co.uk

Just as he said this, what should hap
At the chamber door but a gentle tap?
"Come in!" the Mayor cried, looking bigger;
And in did come the strangest figure!
His queer long coat from heel to head
Was half of yellow and half of red;
And he himself was tall and thin,
With sharp blue eyes each like a pin,
And light loose hair, yet swarthy skin.

Illustrations

Illustrations that accompany poems can be produced in many ways. Large murals can be created in corridors or on external walls or paintings created for display, with text, on display screens. Children can present lunchtime or after school readings / presentations using these images as backdrops. With a data projector, the backdrop might be carefully recorded visual imagery. A series of poems on urban life might be delivered in front of video images made by children of urban landscapes, for example.

Mobiles

Images and words can also be combined in large mobiles. Although these can be displayed in classrooms, the really big ones demand an entrance hall or main school hall for best display. Pieces of thick card should be cut to a variety of shapes (often determined by the subject of the poem) and key phrases and images created / glued on the cards. The components are then suspended from bamboo canes of varying lengths. Most spaces have an ambient draught so it should turn without assistance. Failing this, a stationary (and out of reach) fan can be used to make the images move. If bright colours are used, simple lighting can add effect. Music, or a recording of children speaking the whole poem can be used to accompany the images.

You should have heard the Hamelin people
Ringing the bells till they rocked the steeple;
"Go', cried the Mayor, 'and get long poles!
Poke out the nests and block up the holes.'

Mini-books

Children can produce mini-books of poems, with or without illustrations. Images can be scanned in and manipulated with text and the whole spiral bound. An annual anthology of pupils' poems (edited by class members) can be a useful addition to the bookshelves and sold at cost price to parents.

Challenges and competitions

It is important that children come to see themselves as poets and that poems are not just things that others produce. Schools should therefore promote student poetry and achievement. We are used to seeing children being congratulated for academic or sporting success. How about a fortnightly prize for the best poem with the judging panel comprising representatives of different classes? Competitions such as 'the best limerick/clerihew/ballad' can promote poetry and give children understanding of different forms of poetry. The first line of a limerick can be announced in assembly 'There was a young man from Japan' and children encouraged to hand in potential second lines by a given deadline. The chosen second line is announced a week later 'There was a young man from Japan, Whose verses they never would scan' with invitations to complete line three 'There was a young man from Japan, whose verses they never would scan, When asked why this was, he said it's because' with the final line chosen in week four and the four authors doing a combined reading to the school:

There was a young man from Japan
Whose verses they never would scan
When asked why this was, he said it's because
I always try to get as many words into the last line as I
possibly can.

Such mini-competitions could be linked to national events – National Poetry Day, for example (see: http://poetrysociety.org.uk/index.htm).

Pupil poet laureate

A pupil poet laureate could be created. This promotes the notion of poetry as an important element of school life. The laureate is commissioned to produce poems for special occasions, e.g. teacher retirement, the arrival of new staff and pupils, the planting of a new tree or the cutting down of a diseased one, or the arrival of the bulldozers to begin work on the extension. Some schools nominate a 'poet of the month'.

Teacher as poet

It is important that teachers 'practise what they preach' so they should write poems and perform them to the class and to the school. Often, this will be done in co-operation with their pupils. Messages about the positive role of poetry are carried implicitly within the teacher's attitudes, behaviour and relationship with their own poetry as well as that of their pupils.

Poems as starting points

Poems – children's and those of poets from outside the school – can be important starting points for other creative work, e.g. as a stimulus for short story writing, visual art, drama or dance. Poems can become an essential part of the school day by inviting pupils to present a poem during registration time, or before home time. Rather than using a bell, how about reading a short poem – a limerick perhaps – over the school tannoy to signal the end of a lesson. For more ideas on how to embed poems in the school day, see http://www.poetrysociety.org.uk/npd/events02.htm.

Visiting poets

Teachers can discover who are the poets in the surrounding community and invite them into school to share their work. It is best if this is a balanced activity with pupils presenting their poems as well as experiencing those of the guests. For advice on finding poets, see http://poetrylibrary.org.uk/poetry/remote/edu/txtresou.html. A special day of poetry can be arranged with guests, pupils, parents, siblings (particularly those who have moved on to secondary school) and staff contributing. Such days can receive publicity in local papers with selected poems included in the text. A local paper may be persuaded to run a weekly or monthly 'poetry spot' in which a poem from your school is published, together with a photograph and short biography of the poet.

Performance tours

Poetry performances (poetry shows) can be taken to other schools. This works best if the host school also has something to share with their guests. A poetry festival that involves children from several schools – a secondary school hosting student poets from its feeder primaries, for example – can be an excellent framework for bringing together different age groups to celebrate poetry. Children can also create poetry shows for targeted audiences, e.g. the local playgroup or retirement home, the garden club or Women's Institute.

CHAPTER 6

Common queries

'It's important to develop the adults as well; otherwise they find a poem, chant it out and insult it.'
Jane Griffiths, Headteacher

How do I involve some very diffident children?

Sometimes children can be reluctant performers. It is important to let them choose when to enter the water and then help them develop strokes. The following strategies can help. A shy child could:

- perform actions only as another child recites words;
- join in with a group of voices;
- provide sound effects – the fish gave a terrible sneeze 'ACHOOOOOO' – as another child performs. As this involves careful listening, the child is engaged;
- join a group of regular performers e.g. poetry / drama club;
- control some of the technical aspects.

Any tips on learning lines?

It is easy to underestimate the amount even young children can learn by rote, but take care that 'wooden learning' does not dictate the development of a 'wooden performance.' Is is important that pupils absorb the poem's structure and story rather than thinking of it as a collection of words. Any drama or movement work supports this. The following are all useful strategies:

- give actions to go with particular lines;
- draw a line on the floor. Stand the children in line and chunk poem, going down the line. Everyone knows when it is their turn and has a manageable piece to recite;
- display each section of a poem in front of those who speak it, then substitute paper on which key words are written, then nothing!
- learn by rote yourself – this demonstrates engagement and means that you can make eye contact as you teach;

- encourage children to learn poems for homework and then give a few moments for them to perform to the class;
- have buddies, prompting each other;
- display lines of a poem in the class: a new line each day until the poem is complete.

How do I select appropriate poems?

Eventually children will select their own poems, but to begin with it is important that you have a wide range of resources including classics and raps, for example. Most children's libraries have poems categorised in topics. Finding appropriate ones depends upon the teacher's knowledge of the children – what they are interested in and how effective they are as readers. When children produce their own poems, bind them into books for the school shelves so that they are published poets too and their poems can be read and selected by others.

Look at the chapter 'Recommended texts' (page 70) and don't forget the extremely useful websites (inside back cover).

How can I fit poetry performance into an overcrowded curriculum?

Easily. It is clearly prescribed in the NC and NLS. You may need some flexibility with the literacy hour. You could, for example, have a week of lessons with shorter shared time, more independent time for practice, plenaries for work in progress and a final performance on Friday.

Poetry can be used across the curriculum – in music, dance, drama and history – by work on understanding other times and cultures, for example. A history or geography project may well include researching literature of a time and place and this could be performed as a presentation of all that has been learnt.

How can I help children project their voices?

- The crucial element is the ownership of the poem by the child. If it remains 'someone else's poem from a book', it is much more difficult for the child to treat it with confidence and physical and vocal attack. Getting them to illustrate or reproduce it in some way may help this process.
- All poems are meant to be spoken aloud, so most are not private events. Realising and experiencing this as early as possible makes speaking poems less 'unusual' and the children's delivery less self-conscious.
- Even young children can be encouraged to develop mummy, daddy and baby bear voices so that they speak the same poem in different ways.
- Pairs or groups can work independently in a large space such as the hall or playground where there is a distance between the performer and the listener(s) who signal if they find it difficult to hear.
- 'Moving a poem' often produces a vocal energy that standing still does not.
- Make poems part of everyday school time. Invite children to read or speak a poem in registration time, for example.
- Use electronic amplification if children are reading in a big room to lots of others.

How can I encourage children to work in role?

- Model this yourself. Teacher in Role can be a powerful focus for teaching engagement and imaginative response.
- Use dramatic techniques such as hot seating as a preparation for performance.
- Simple props such as a variety of hats can help.
- Writing in role as part of preparation takes children inside the poem.

Who should I involve?

A good question. The scope is potentially enormous. Possibilities include:

- the community. Often parents/governors are pleased to help with productions and even appear in them themselves. The thread of literary heritage is dramatically portrayed when players include the very old to the very young;
- librarians are good at tracing information. Your local library should carry details of arts organisations such as regional arts organisations which can advise you, for example, of performance poets in the area. Two useful reference books usually found in libraries are *A guide to Children's Poetry for Teachers and Librarians* by B. Wade (Scholar Press 1996), which is a comprehensive guide to poetry collections, audio tapes and poetry contacts, and *Where's that poem?* by H. Morris (Simon and Schuster Education 1992), which has an index of 1000 authors and details suitable poems in subject categories, e.g. circuses, lost lovers. This should be an indispensable book in every school library;
- the whole school. This ensures progression, interest and confidence;
- other schools who might like to be involved in a Poetry Day, for example, where schools or classes come together to celebrate their performances;
- the drama department in a local school of education may be pleased to send a poetry show or set up a workshop using tutors and students.

CHAPTER 7

Recommended texts

'Lists of books are useless. We don't do them. You need to see a book
to know if it's any good or not.'
(Bookseller at UKLA Conference, 2003)

Poems come from many places. Children bring them to school; some of them they have read, some of them they've made up; some of them they have always known; some are chanted in the playground - where have these come from? Nobody knows.

Children's own poems are often performed spontaneously in play; I bring to mind a Japanese infant in a punt in Cambridge. To the amusement of all aboard she stood confidently in the shade of her family's parasols and began to recite:

Row row row the boat
gently down the stream

with her hands on swaying hips. The language she used was a mixture of Japanese and English. It was a performance. It is possible to have an instant poetry performance from poems children already know but, given that a function of school is to enlarge pupils' repertoires, new texts are important. The range available is exciting and very varied. It includes the internet (see Chapter 4). Teachers' professional magazines often carry poetry posters with interesting ideas for performance but most poems are to be found in books. Given that booklists are of limited use we have not included them but instead reviewed some of the best texts that could support poetry performance. However it is important that children find their own poems as a community of performers. Teachers can guide taste but not dictate it.

Anthologies

All The Best, The Selected Poems Of Roger McGough, Penguin 2003 ISBN 0-670-91418-5
All would agree this is a classic for connoisseurs and those on the way to connoisseurship. So many opportunities to chant, sing, whisper, shout, deliberate, pause; become a mafia cat, a crocodile farmer, a little wooden dummy.

Cars Stars Electric Guitars by James Carter, Walker Books 2002 ISBN 0-7445-8635-6
An exciting collection of poems from a newish poet with an eclectic style; there are Rosen-style wonderings aloud, clever word play and conversations that give the opportunity for dialogues with various voices. *Rhyming with Orange* is an example of a funny and sophisticated poem with opportunities for clever timing and extension into a chain poem. Suitable for key stages 1 and 2.

Family Phantom by Gervaise Phinn, Puffin 2003 ISBN 0-141-31446-x
Witty, riddlesome, spooky, exciting Phinn wins over the reader to the ways of poetry. Creative language play abounds to tease the young performer. There are many opportunities for whole class chanting for example in the description of *The Loch Ness Monster*. Suitable for both key stages 1 and 2.

How To Make A Snail Fall In Love With You And Other Surprising Poems by Lindsay Macrae, Penguin 2003 ISBN 0-14-131430-3
The themes of these poems can obsess primary pupils: fallouts, embarrassing dads, moving to another table, divorce, having to eat everything on your plate. Here they are recognised, witticised, made into something we all understand. Lots of opportunities to perform in the first person, for example *The Fallout*. Most suitable for key stage 2.

I've Got A Poem For You: Poems To Perform collected by John Foster, Oxford University Press 2001 ISBN 0 19 276256 7
Perhaps only a performance poet could have made such a collection poems which beg to be brought to life with the human voice. There is so much here that could enthuse children from both key stages. Some are written for more than one voice – for example, Gareth Owen's irrepressibly funny poem *Excuses, Excuses.*

Other poems challenge children to master another English such as Benjamin Zephaniah's *Talking Turkeys*; *Rat it Up* by Adrian Mitchell is a wonderful invitation to be a real cool rapper. Not all the poems are funny – many are thought-provoking or tell dramatic tales such as Kipling's

A Smuggler's Song, a classic for a community of young performance poets.

One Hundred Years of Poetry for Children by Michael Harrison and Christopher Stuart-Clark, Oxford University Press 1999 ISBN 0 19 276258-3
Thought-provoking, humorous and moving poetry written over the last century. Some of the works are written for children, for example T.S. Eliot's *Preludes*, but it is important that they hear works which will become part of their repertoire as adults. This is a book for older children which contains mainly longer poems some of which would lend themselves to dramatisation such as de la Mare's *The Listeners*.

Poems to annoy your parents, chosen by Susie Gibbs, Oxford University Press 2003 ISBN 0 19 276290-7
This book warns the reader, 'Any performance of these poems is undertaken at the reader's own risk' and directs 'Find a suitably safe and out of the reach position and/or establish a getaway route . . . read a few poems aloud to your parents. Take cover..' There is a real incentive to learn the poems off by heart and many are suitable for chanting, for example Peter Dixon's poem, *Father's yelling*.

Others are modern classics such as Alfred Noyes' poem, *Daddy fell into the pond*. All the works are funny, easy to learn and would appeal to both key stages.

Poems to freak out your teachers, chosen by Susie Gibbs, Oxford University Press 2003 ISBN 019 276292 3
This is the sort of book children bring to school. It is irreverent, for example *Our Teacher*, and cosily subversive: children patter ink pellets, pick their noses and torment teachers who get very, very cross. It will tempt even diffident children to perform as there are short, patterned poems which are easy to memorise and chant and poems which demand intonation – for example, Mc Gough's poem *On and On . . .* which is a series of questions. Poets including Allan Ahlberg, Brian Patten and Colin McNaughton make a book which could enthuse key stages 1 and 2.

Poems for Everyone: A Treasury of Poems about People, collected by Michael Harrison and Christopher Stuart-Clark, Oxford University Press 2001 ISBN 0192762486, £12.99
Poems about all kinds of people including many about families, Mum, Dad, my little sister, twin sisters, new baby – they are all there brought to

life by some of the best: Spike Milligan, Kit Wright, Roger McGough, Carol Anne Duffy, WH Auden. A book for older children with some profound work which will challenge the able language user as well as fun poems which are stylistically original. *The Sound Collector* by Roger Mc Gough would be wonderful to overlay with sound effects. More suitable for key stage 2.

Spollyolly-diddlyitis: The Doctor Book by Michael Rosen, illustrated by Quentin Blake, Walker Books 2000 ISBN 0-7445-7765-9
Part of a series of thin, themed books (other titles include *Hard-Boiled Legs, The Breakfast Book* and *Smelly Jelly Smelly Fish* – all written by Michael Rosen and illustrated by Quentin Blake) which contain a variety of poems – long, short, all funny, some poignant. The laconic Rosen style gives children the chance to practise being urbane and whimsical as they narrate some of the situations in which characters find themselves when going to the doctor's. Conversations between patients and parents or doctors give the opportunity for dramatic readings with more than one character and the 'Things we Say' feature in all the books could form the basis of a chain poem. Suitable for key stages 1 and 2.

The Kingfisher Book of Comic Verse, Selected by Roger McGough, Kingfisher Books, London, 1986 ISBN 086272179
Really popular with children, this could provide material for many performances. It is organised into themes – seasons, fair warnings, meet the folks – and contains some of the doyens of the 70s and 80s children's poetry scene: McGough himself, Allan Ahlberg, Gareth Owen, Michael Rosen, Brian Patten as well as classic work by long established authors: Ogden Nash, Walter de La Mare and writers not normally associated with children's work: Carol Anne Duffy, Philip Larkin and Mike Harding. Some works are witty; some profound; some revolting – they are all funny. Many classrooms must have this book, dilapidated from overuse. Suitable for key stages 1 and 2.

The Bee's Knees Roger McGough Penguin London 2003 ISBN 0-14-131495-8
Variously described as 'the best known and loved poet on the street', 'an international ambassador for poetry' McGough has put together new and exciting poems which beg to be read aloud, for example the deceptively simple Glug. Many of the poems would make scaffolds for children's own chain poems. Suitable for key stages 1 and 2.

The Oxford Treasury Of Classic Poems, selected by Michael Harrison and Christopher Stuart-Clark, Oxford University Press 2002

ISBN 0 19 276289-3.
As the title suggests the best are here: Tennyson, Keats, Belloc and Betjeman herald the more modern poets such as Causley, McGough and Hughes. Older children who can learn longer texts could dramatically stage narrative works such as the *Lady of Shalott* by Tennyson, *The Highwayman* by Alfred Noyes, *The Terrible Path* by Brian Patten and *The Adventures of Isabel* by Ogden Nash. Most suitable for key stage 2.

There's An Awful Lot of Weirdos In Our Neighbourhood: a Book Of Rather Silly Poems And Pictures, by Colin McNaughton, Walker Books 2000 ISBN 0-7445-7778-0
This has become a classic since it was first published in 1987. Very funny poems that children love: irreverent, easy to learn and with clever use of language. There are many which are suitable for more than one voice. Suitable for key stages 1 and 2.

Under The Moon And Over The Sea: A Collection Of Caribbean Poems, edited by John Agard and Grace Nichols, Walker Books 2002
ISBN 0-7445-3736-3
Sooo good! Pictures of full Caribbean moon nights when blue crabs come out of their holes, weird non-Eurocentric characters; Anancy, Jumbie Man, Duppy Dan, Mama-Wata, proverbs that highlight other ways of living, they're all there, penned and collected by the elite of Caribbean poets. Children have the opportunity to experiment with the patois, for example the rhythmic *Duppy Dan* by John Agard. Suitable for key stages 1 and 2.

Wish You Were Here (And I Wasn't): a Book of Poems and Pictures for Globe Trotters, by Colin McNaughton, Walker Books 2000
ISBN 0-7445-7755-4
Dramatic and funny. Five minutes leafing through the pages immediately suggests various ways of presenting these poems as there are opportunities for chaining, chorusing, chanting. Suitable for key stages 1 and 2.

Because a fire was in my head edited by Michael Morpurgo, Faber and Faber 2001
ISBN 0-571-20583-6
Morpurgo has always loved poetry; from the early playground chants of his childhood to the classic writers, some of whose work he grew to love as a young child listening to his mother. There is a milky way of starred poems: the biblical, classics, anonymous jingles which grew without penning, through to the new wave poets. They could all resonate in the primary school. Suitable for key stages 1 and 2.